The Complete Guide to Personal Finance

For Teenagers and College Students

Revised 2nd Edition with Workbook On Companion CD

By Tamsen Butler

With Foreword By Darlene Gudrie Butts,
veteran financial adviser and author of
Lessons from the Depression:
Eliminating Debt the Old-Fashioned Way

THE COMPLETE GUIDE TO PERSONAL FINANCE FOR TEENAGERS
AND COLLEGE STUDENTS REVISED 2ND EDITION WITH WORKBOOK
ON COMPANION CD

Copyright © 2016 Atlantic Publishing Group, Inc.
1405 SW 6th Avenue • Ocala, Florida 34471 • Phone 352-622-1825 • Fax 352-622-1875
Website: www.atlantic-pub.com • E-mail: sales@atlantic-pub.com
SAN Number: 268-1250

Library of Congress Cataloging-in-Publication Data

Butler, Tamsen, 1974- author.
  The complete guide to personal finance : for teenagers and college students / Tamsen Butler.
-- Revised 2nd edition.
     pages cm
  "With Workbook On Companion CD."
  Includes bibliographical references and index.
  ISBN 978-1-62023-070-1 (alk. paper) -- ISBN 1-62023-070-4 (alk. paper) 1.
Teenagers--Finance, Personal. 2. College students--Finance, Personal. 3. Finance, Personal.
I. Title.
  HG179.B877 2015
  332.02400835--dc23
                        2015033899

Printed in the United States

Over the years, we have adopted a number of dogs from rescues and shelters. First there was Bear and after he passed, Ginger and Scout. Now, we have Kira, another rescue. They have brought immense joy and love not just into our lives, but into the lives of all who met them.

We want you to know a portion of the profits of this book will be donated in Bear, Ginger and Scout's memory to local animal shelters, parks, conservation organizations, and other individuals and nonprofit organizations in need of assistance.

– Douglas & Sherri Brown,
President & Vice-President of Atlantic Publishing

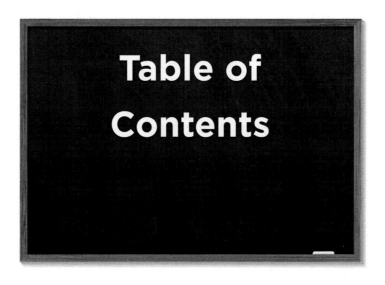

Chapter 5:
Creditors and the Games They Play   129

The Principles of Credit..130

The Tactics 135

Chapter 6: Debt, Debt, and More Debt   161

Good Debt and Bad Debt...163

Chapter 11:
Everything Else You Need to Know 243

Chapter 12: On Your Own 249

Conclusion: Congratulations! 255

Glossary of Terms 257

Author Biography 277

Bibliography 279

Index 281

Foreword

Trying to figure out the money game can be challenging for anyone, let alone a teenager or young adult. There are so many concepts to learn, and most often, those concepts are interpreted by teens as boring or complicated. Many parents do not feel competent to teach personal finance, and it is not a subject taught in school. Couple that with the fact that 60 percent of bachelor's degree recipients borrow to fund their education and 84 percent of undergraduate students have at least one credit card, and you have a disaster waiting to happen.

This book is trying to change that trend. Tamsen Butler, in *The Complete Guide to Personal Finance: For Teenagers and College Students REVISED 2nd Edition*, seems to do the impossible. This book provides a proper education in personal finance in an entertaining and understandable manner.

The purpose of this book is not to tell the readers what to do, but to educate them on the various options and the possible results of one's choices. Even if all of the information is not relevant to your current situation, this book can be used as a reference for each financial stage of the early adult years. It is comprehensive and user-friendly, and it is sprinkled with real-life anecdotes that illustrate each financial concept. Anyone can benefit from this approach to teaching personal financial planning.

As a veteran financial adviser and author of *Lessons from the Depression: Eliminating Debt the Old-Fashioned Way*, I found the information in this book extremely helpful in conveying the concepts a teenager or college student needs for a financially successful life. For those students who are looking for information on their own, or parents who want to find a guide that will teach fundamental financial concepts, this book will teach you everything you need to know. Butler has done a great job of writing an easy-to-read and informative book on a subject that all can benefit from.

Darlene Gudrie Butts

Veteran Financial Adviser
Author of *Lessons from the Depression: Eliminating Debt the Old-Fashioned Way*
www.lessonsfromthedepression.net

Darlene Gudrie Butts has been a financial adviser for over 23 years and has authored *Lessons from the Depression: Eliminating Debt the Old-Fashioned Way*. Her goal is to educate the world on personal financial concepts one reader at a time. Her second book, *The Ripple Effect: A Guide for Parents, Teachers and Coaches*, came out in the spring of 2010.

Introduction

C hances are, you already have a lot on your mind. You have to keep up with your school work, extra activities that quickly take up most of your free time, and relationships with your friends and family that fill up the rest of your schedule. Do you really need the extra burden of learning about something that doesn't even seem to be a big deal right now? Why should you bother worrying about the ins and outs of personal finance when you already have enough to worry about?

Besides, isn't finance *boring*?

There are a few reasons why you should learn how to handle your money now. You're in a great position to learn because, as a student, you are accustomed to learning new things and haven't already developed bad financial habits. Also, as a young adult, you've likely begun to crave independence. Managing money on your own is an excellent first step toward becoming independent from your parents. First and foremost, however, you need to know that effectively handling your money is a talent that will serve you well for the rest of your life. No matter where you go in life — whether you become an artist, a doctor, an undercover agent for the Secret Service, or a stay-at-home parent — money will always come into play in your daily decisions. Will you have enough money to own the car you want to drive? Will you be able to take vacations with your family? Will you be able to cover day-to-day expenses? If you can master the art of basic personal finance in your teenage years, you will have all the tools you need to effectively manage your money now and far into the future.

Personal finance does not have to be boring. This book will not drone on about annuity investments or the foreign exchange market. Instead, you will learn the basics so you don't have to add "money" to the long list of things you already have to worry about. After all, if you can figure this stuff out now, you already have a leg up on plenty of adults who fumble around with money for their entire lives.

As a teenager, you have the distinct advantage of having time on your side. You can do amazing things with relatively small amounts of money if you start now. Whether you bought this book on your own, or an adult gave it to you as a gift hoping you will take an interest in your financial future, prepare to have fun — while also learning how to take control of your money.

Are you asking yourself how money could possibly be interesting and fun? Once you realize that understanding your finances isn't really so difficult, and that you can easily manage your own finances doing the things you probably already do (spending time online or toying with your cell phone), maybe you will decide it is worth it to learn more about managing your money.

The organization of the book is fairly simple. The personal finance concepts get a bit more difficult as you read through the book — with the basics up front and specifics on moving out on your own toward the end. Case studies from finance professionals and real-life stories from teens and college students are presented throughout. A helpful glossary of finance-related terms is included at the end of the book.

Are you ready to learn everything you need to know about personal finance? Let's get started.

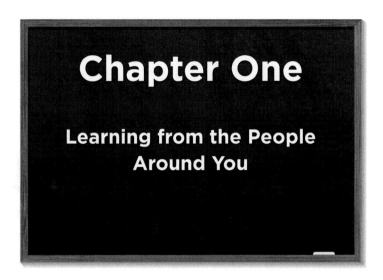

Chapter One

Learning from the People Around You

There is a man who lives near Moab, Utah who has sworn off money. He lives in a cave, scavenges for food, and refuses to use money at all. If people insist on giving him money, he either gives it to someone else or leaves the cash somewhere for someone else to find it. He has no job, no income, no insurance, and claims to be completely happy with the life he has chosen. He actually isn't the first person in modern society to do this, but he might be the most famous because he maintains a blog about his lifestyle by using the computer free of charge at the local library.

Find Out More

Want to learn more about the man who lives without money? Visit his blog at **www.zerocurrency.blogspot.com**.

This is probably in stark contrast to the people you know. Imagine if this is how you were raised — by parents who swore off money and who had no desire whatsoever for material possessions. Do you think this would change the way you think about money, or do you think the quest for cash and material goods is something we are all born with?

The truth is, you are always influenced by the people around you, whether you realize it or not. The way your friends and family deal with money has a huge effect on how you deal with money. Problems arise when the people around you aren't managing their personal finances like they should. Because of these bad habits, you might assume it is completely normal to be broke, have bill collectors calling your house, or charge up credit cards for things you don't really need (but you really want).

The people around you can teach you valuable lessons about personal finance, whether they manage their own money effectively, or they spend it with reckless abandon every chance they get. Always keep in mind: You have the power to manage your personal finances with finesse, even if the people around you don't have that particular talent.

Your Parents

If you're lucky, your parents not only effectively manage their personal finances, but have also taken the time to teach you everything you need to know about money. There is a good chance, though, your parents may not have a solid grasp on their finances. The average household has credit card debt, does not have enough money in a savings account to get them through a few months without an income should they lose their job, and may even be a couple of paychecks away from huge financial problems.

Have you ever had a serious talk with your parents about personal finance? You have probably learned quite a few things about money just by watching them, whether it's the fact that there is never enough money or the strict guideline that a portion of your income always goes into a savings account. If you have not had an intentional discussion with your parents about personal finance, though, you may be confused about some of the ways they handle money. Do you wonder about the bills that come to your house? Do you wonder if there is enough money set aside for you to attend college? Do you wonder about why your parents spend money the way they do?

Personal finance can be a touchy subject with parents. First of all, they certainly do not want to look like they aren't managing their money well, especially in the eyes of their child. They want to be a good example, so they may not be eager to talk with you about the money problems they had last month, or the amount of money they have sitting in an investment account for retirement. On the other hand, you can learn quite a bit from your parents when it comes to managing money. If they are willing to talk about their finances with you, you should be eager to sit down and have the discussion.

Ask your parents about how much money they have in savings. Ask them about what bills they must pay every month, and how much money they have left over after the bills are paid. How do they balance their checkbook? How do they make sure they have the money they need so they can pay all the bills and still have money left over for fun purchases? If your parents have a written budget, ask them to share it with you and explain to you how they set the budget and what changes they would like to make.

Again, be aware that not all parents want to talk about money with their child. Allowing you to take a hard look at their finances can make some parents feel like they are revealing a huge failure. The truth is, most adults feel like they don't earn enough money, are too deeply in debt, or don't have enough money in savings. This can be embarrassing for parents, especially if they feel as though they don't manage their personal finances very well. For this reason, keep in mind, if your parents flat out refuse to give you a peek at how they manage their finances, it probably isn't because they do not think you will understand any of it; it's probably because they just don't want to show you something they usually consider to be private and may be a little uncomfortable to discuss. If your parents won't talk to you about their finances, you can't force them to, but you may want to find another trusted adult who will feel comfortable talking to you about their money situation.

CASE STUDY: GETTING READY FOR THE FUTURE

Jessica — High School Student

When I think of finances, I think of fretted faces, shaky hands, clenched pens, wrinkles spread throughout foreheads strategically creating a picture of perfect confusion, and the infamous torn envelopes with prices enfolded with sums too great to dream of affording. Bills have never been man's best friend. Therefore, as a high school student, when I see my dad with bills scattered across our kitchen table, I get a gut-wrenching feeling — that feeling of "soon that is going to be me and all of my own responsibility." At that moment when the epiphany struck, I started feeling claustrophobic with all the outside pressures of part-time jobs, scholarships, loans, and money to support my thriving social life. Thus, leading to an important question to all of us teens: Where do I start?!

I am not the perfect child who always has all the answers to perfectly balanced finances. I have learned, and am still learning, that I need a specific financial plan, or I will spend beyond my afforded boundaries. I have been taught to save. I know it sounds cliché, but now is the opportune time.

College may be the main focus directed at us when saving is tossed into the conversation. Although it is highly important to save for college, it isn't the only aspect of life in which saving applies. Speaking from personal experience, within these last couple years, I have saved and worked to participate in week-long mission trips. Within a period of a few months, I had to gather $1,100. This, as a sophomore in high school, is quite a sum; however, for a mission trip, I was blessed the amount was not higher.

You might be inquiring as to how in the world I scrounged up that particular amount of green. I — maybe not as much as I should have — cut back on activities and fundraised. If my friends asked me to go out to the movies, dinner, and then bowling, I would just go bowling. Or, sometimes, I wouldn't go hang out at all that Friday night, but instead, I put back the money toward the trip to Honduras or Ecuador. Knowing cutting back on activities would not cover the total expense, I fundraised. I worked bake sales, sold chocolate bars, washed cars, and so much more. I learned that with whatever activity in life, you need to work as hard as you can and save in every way possible. I recommend to any teenager to grasp the concept now instead of waiting until the moment of desperation comes. Why not get a head start and save money, instead of waiting and attempting to pay a large sum from your wallet at once — if you decide to live the latter, then all you will accomplish is being broke. Make life easier — save!

How to ask for a peek

Because personal finances can be a delicate subject with some parents, you should ask permission before you snatch the checkbook and start thumbing through it, or before you start opening bills that come in the mail. Instead, approach your parents and tell them you are ready to learn more about the family finances and ask if they are willing to sit down with you and give you a peek at how the household money comes and goes.

Don't be shocked if your parents squirm a little at the thought of allowing you access to the family's finances. Some parents will always see their kids as their babies no matter how old the kids get, so asking to learn about the family's finances may come as a surprise. Cut your parents some slack. After all, they *did* change your diapers at one point.

It is a good idea to have some questions ready beforehand when your parents agree to show you the status of the family finances. Don't just sit there and expect them to present you with all the information you need. Instead, ask questions like:

- How do you decide how much money to spend each month?
- How much money do you save each month?
- What expenses do you use a credit card for? Why?
- What is the best personal finance advice you can give me?
- What are some mistakes you have made with your money?

Hardly any parent can honestly make the claim that they have never made any monetary mistakes. Even though their worst mistakes may date back to their college days, chances are, your parents once fumbled around with money problems before they figured out how to manage their finances. You can learn a lot from the financial mistakes your parents made, whether the mistakes were made a week or several years ago.

Learning by example

No, parents don't know everything. How many times have you thought to yourself, "I will never, ever wind up like my parents?" It doesn't matter if it is their sense of style you never want to imitate or their taste in music you do not understand. You already know your parents don't have all the answers to everything, but they do know a thing or two about running a family.

Take the example your parents give for what it is: an example of one way to manage personal finances for a family, no matter right or wrong. It doesn't matter if your parents don't have all the answers or if their personal financial management isn't dazzling. What matters is they're offering you a realistic look into what personal finances can look like when you hit adulthood. You should decide whether it's an example of something you want to some-day become — or an example of something you want to avoid.

Other People

Everyone around you has their own way of dealing with mon-ey. Have you ever seen a teacher drive up to school in a flashy car and wondered how much it cost? Or, maybe your friend has complained to you about not having enough money to go to the movies to see a new release. Personal finances — and how we manage them — are common, everyday topics, even if we don't talk about them intentionally. You may not realize you pick up cues from everyone around you regarding how they deal with money, but you really do.

If your friends have access to money, how do they handle it? They probably fall into one of three categories:

- **Spender**: As soon as this friend has any money, it's usual-ly gone. Sometimes it seems like this friend has no control over money whatsoever.

- **Saver**: This friend always seems to have money stashed away, but rarely spends the money on anything unless there has been careful consideration first.

- **Combination**: This friend is a mixture of the other two categories; this friend spends money, but also saves. They have a perfect balance between spending and saving. This friend seems to have a good handle on money.

What category do your closest friends fall into? There is a good chance you pick up on how your friends handle their money, and they may even influence how you handle your own finances. Suppose you are at the mall with some of your friends. Everyone else gets in line to buy a $4 smoothie — or, worse, a $6 coffee — but you had not planned on spending money on anything besides clothes. What do you do? Do you allow your friends to influence you into buying an expensive drink? Your friends may not even try to influence you on purpose, but it is amazing how influential the people around us can be. You may see your friend with something, like that $4 smoothie, and even though you had no desire to have a smoothie when you first walked into the mall, seeing your friend with the smoothie made you want one, too. You're easily influenced by your friends because you spend so much time with them, and also because you probably care what they think. Everyone wants to be accepted — whether they are 15 or 55.

Is there something wrong with buying a $4 drink at the mall when you hadn't planned on making this purchase? Not necessarily. Is there anything wrong with buying the same things your friends buy? Not always. The trick is to know when you are making purchases only because the people around you are making purchases. Don't worry: Adults who have plenty of years of experience dealing with personal finances still have this problem. How many adults do you know drive expensive cars but don't seem to have enough money for anything else? It isn't something only teens or young adults deal with. And actually, you have an advantage over these adults. You are at an age where you can make the decision early to buy things because you need or want them, instead of because everyone around you is buying. If you can make this decision now, you will save yourself quite a bit of money in the long run.

The next time you go out with your friends, pay attention to how each of them spends their money. Are they making good decisions, or are they spending with reckless abandon? You don't have to analyze every dime, but if you pay attention, it will become obvious that everyone has a spending style. Some people buy impulsively, some people buy compulsively, and some people hardly spend at all. If you can figure out how — and, more importantly, why — the people closest to you spend money, you will probably notice a trend that is similar to how you spend your own money. Like it or not, we're influenced by the people around us.

You can learn a lot about personal finances from the people around you, but these lessons aren't always examples you will want to follow. You should begin to recognize when the people around you are influencing how you spend your money, and if that influence isn't positive, you can nip it in the bud and make financial decisions that are best for you.

CASE STUDY: THE IMPORTANCE OF SAVING

Christy — High School Student

Growing up, my dad always had some assortment of pocket change he would empty out and let me play with and count. That fascination of change was the beginning of my obsession to save. I'll find unwanted change lying around, especially pennies, and pick it up and put it in one of my many piggy banks, which are organized according to the value of the coin. I've learned eventually it will add up. So as soon as I fill up a piggy bank, I transfer the money into my savings account, which I opened when I was in elementary school. Every dollar I get from a birthday or Christmas also goes into the account. At this rate, you'd think I'd have thousands... but I don't.

I love having the security of knowing I have money if I need it. But I have a habit of dipping into my account, although it's rarely ever for me. I like to buy my closest friends and family members gifts when it is appropriate. However, that in particular isn't what makes my account dwindle. It's life. The economy is falling to pieces, which doesn't my help the fact that my family already lives paycheck to paycheck. So, of course, when mom needs gas money, my account is all-access. She hates borrowing money from her own daughter more than anything in the world, but I always insist that it's OK because wherever the money is going, it's going to benefit me in some way or another. Because of the low income in my household, I pay for items that are not essential, like my yearbooks or electronics, out of my own expenses.

I personally don't have a steady source of income, aside from the holidays; I have no job. This is why I'm applying for a job at the summer camp that I've been volunteering at for a couple of years. I would like to have a job during the school year, but that would be impossible under my circumstances. I live in a town an hour away from my school; my evenings and weekends are consumed with homework and just taking life in when I get the chance. The only way I'm even able to get to my school is because my Grandpa happened to get a new vehicle at the time I was looking for a cheap car. He graciously gave his old one to me (an act for which I am forever grateful). And in that hour drive to and from school each day, I am accompanied by the four other people I carpool with, who pay me weekly. This money goes toward gas, and whenever I have a little leftover, I try to save it to get my account back on track. I guess you could say I'm just a yellow paint job away from being called a taxi driver.

I think I'm on the right track as far as being able to manage finances. I know saving is good, and I love saving. And last, I know having a job is a good direction to take, and I have the ambition to get one.

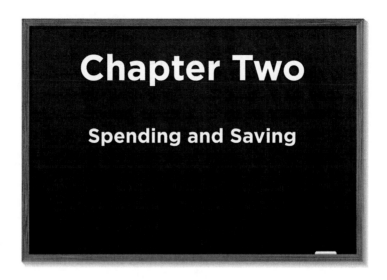

Chapter Two

Spending and Saving

Personal finance concepts become a lot easier when you realize it all boils down to two things: spending and saving. In other words, what do you do with money once you have it in your hands? Do you run out and buy whatever catches your eye, or do you make purchases you have planned for beforehand? Do you buy things you need, or do you buy things you want? Does any of your money go into a piggybank or savings account, or is it gone before you can even consider putting some of it away?

In other words, what do you do with the money you get?

Here is the great thing about your money: *You're in charge*. You get to tell it what to do and where to go. Unless your parents put restrictions on how you use your money, it is your show — and you're running it.

Needs versus Wants

"Need versus want" is a common phrase in personal finance. These three words sum up a simple concept many people have a hard time mastering, even long into adulthood. You are supposed to buy the things you need and wait to buy the things you want until you can afford to make the purchase. The line between needs and wants can be pretty blurry sometimes, so it is important to learn how to figure out which category a purchase you want to make falls into. Do you need it, or do you want it? You may be surprised to discover a lot of things you think you need are actually things you want, and you don't actually need them after all.

Sometimes, we get so used to all the niceties that come along with living in a modern, prospering society that "wants" start to edge their way into the "needs" category within our minds. For example, you may think that you need a cell phone — after all, you have always had one, and everyone else around you has one— but when it comes right down to it, you may not actually need one. A cell phone is generally not a need; it's a want. Does this mean you shouldn't own a cell phone? No. It means the other things you actually need should come as a priority when you are making a budget and planning your spending. *You will learn more about budgeting in Chapter 4.*

What falls into the category of need? Think of the things you actually need to function within your life. Food is a need. Shelter is a need. Clothing is a need. Keep in mind, though, many of these needs may be met by your parents at this point in your life unless you are already out on your own. For this reason, you

cannot make the claim that a designer-label shirt is a need when you already have a closet full of clothing. By the same token, you can't put late night trips to Taco Bell into the needs category if your parents supply you with a fridge stocked with food at your house. You probably see where this is going already; the needs category is a basic (and somewhat stingy) category that is actually not all that long. As you begin to live life more independently, your needs list will grow quite a bit when you start paying for utilities, food, and shelter, but rest assured, even adults can have a hard time distinguishing between a need and a want.

Need versus wants questionnaire

The following questionnaire is an easy way to figure out if something is a need versus a want. This questionnaire assumes your parents provide you with food and housing, and your main concern is purchasing items for school. Remember: There is nothing wrong with buying something you don't really need, as long as you have budgeted for it and can actually afford it. The point of this questionnaire is not to say you shouldn't buy something; it is only to help you distinguish between a need and a want.

Ask yourself these questions:

1. *Is this purchase something I really need to for school?*

    If the answer is:

    Yes: Keep moving down the list to the next question.

    No: Unless you really need this item for school or some other important reason, this purchase falls into the category of a want.

2. *Can I buy a cheaper version of this item?*

    If the answer is:

    Yes: Cheaper isn't always better, but if you're buying an expensive items just because it's the version everyone else has, this purchase falls into the category of a want.

    No: Keep moving down the list to the next question.

3. *Can I wait to make this purchase?*

    If the answer is:

    Yes: If you don't need to make this purchase right now, but you still want to, this falls into the category of a want.

    No: If you need this item right now, and the two other questions led you here, there is a good chance this purchase falls into the category of a need.

You can revise this questionnaire to work for just about any purchase as not all needs are related to school. After all, you need clothes to wear and food to eat, so use this questionnaire as a quick checklist to figure out if any purchase is a need or a want.

CASE STUDY:
STRETCHING DOLLARS
Stephanie — High School Student

For the majority of my middle and high school years, my family and I have been living on a single-person income. My father cannot work due to major health conditions that cause him a great deal of pain, and he was denied disability insurance. Even though I am physically and legally able to work, I cannot, as I have neither a license nor a car, and we live in the countryside far from potential job locations. The amount of money it would take for gas and the inconvenience it is to drive me all the way into town and back are not worth a part-time, minimum-wage job. Thus, we survive on a salary of approximately $23,000 per annum.

It is not easy. Even on a strict budget, debt lurks just within sight each month. The simple rule we have to follow that governs all expenses: Is it a want or a need?

Priority goes to utilities and other bills, and then the other necessary expenses, like food for ourselves and the animals.

Neither my mom nor I can afford health insurance, and my dad has it only through the VA for his service in the Army (which is fortunate, because he needs it the most). There is also no money in the budget for life insurance, and so clearly, there is no way I can get automobile insurance, so I cannot get my license, let alone a car.

It is difficult, especially when surrounded by those who don't have to worry about money. They can splurge on a nice jacket or go out to eat at a fancy restaurant, and they don't need to worry about college.

However, being on the verge of going out into the real world and facing the realities of college expenses and bills, I have come to realize I wouldn't have had my adolescent years any other way.

Life has been rough, but having to live this way has taught me valuable lessons about life. It's taught me how to differentiate between what is necessary and what is wanted. I know I'm going into the real world with at least some protection, as I will know how to budget and know how to survive on the bare minimum. Many of the aforementioned will doubtless run into trouble and find themselves in debt before long if they continue wasting money with such frivolity when it no longer is coming from their parents, as they never really learned how to save and manage.

But above all, living on such a tight budget has taught me the real value of a dollar and what it means to really work for it, for which I am most grateful.

Why does it matter?

Why should you bother taking such a close look at how you spend your money? The truth is, the way you spend your money has a lot to do with whether or not you can be successful with personal financial management. It may seem like there is a lot more to personal finance than just how you spend your money — and indeed there is a lot more to it — but the basic fundamental concept of not spending your money on things you don't need is a vital concept to grasp. If you can master this concept, you will be sitting pretty with your money throughout your life.

Take a look at two different scenarios to see how even relatively small amounts of money can really add up over time.

Scenario 1: The spender

Josh gets an allowance of $30 per week. His parents cover all his necessary expenses, such as food, shelter, and clothing, so the allowance is his to use however he wants. When he gets his allowance on Friday, he immediately heads off to the mall and buys games for his computer or books he has wanted to read. Any money left over buys sodas and snacks. The only time he saves his allowance is when he wants to buy something that costs more than $30, but his typical weekly ritual is to spend all the money his parents gave him without saving any of the money at all. By Monday, he's usually out of money and must wait until Friday before he can spend any more.

Josh continues to receive this allowance for three years before getting a part-time job. During this time, Josh does not save any money. An allowance of $30 per week may not seem like a lot of money, but within three years, he has received a total of $4,680. That's enough money to buy a decent used car or go on a really great vacation — but Josh did not save any money at all.

What if Josh continues to waste $30 per week throughout his adult life? It isn't a huge amount of money, but it can really add up. By the time he's 65 years old, if he started at age 15, he will have wasted $78,000.

Scenario 2: The saver

Ethan gets the same $30 per week as an allowance from his parents. His parents also cover all of his necessary expenses. Unlike Josh, however, Ethan decides to only spend a portion of his allowance each week and to put the rest into a savings account at the bank. Although the amount of money he saves each week varies depending on what he needs to buy, he saves an average of $15 per week. Because he is so good about saving some money, when something comes along that he really wants to buy, he doesn't have to wait for too long to make the purchase because the money is already in his savings account. Ethan does not make impulse buys very often, and his savings grow quickly.

This pattern continues for three years until he get a part-time job. Within that time span, he put approximately $2,340 into a savings account. Because Ethan decided to put his money into a savings account that earns interest (you will learn more about savings accounts and interest in Chapter 3), he earned even more money. In three years, with an interest rate of 3 percent, his savings account has a balance of $2,460.

Suppose Ethan continued the practice of putting $15 a week into his savings account throughout his adult life, starting at age 15 and continuing until age 65. It isn't a lot of money, and most people won't even notice having $15 less to spend each week. By the time he is ready to stop working and retire around age 65, though, this small weekly deposit will grow into $39,000. Assuming his savings earns interest at a rate of 3 percent, it has the potential to grow to approximately $90,000, in large part due to the interest the money earns when it sits in the bank.

Personal finance doesn't always have to involve large amounts of money. As a teen, time is on your side. Even a small amount of money can equal big bucks down the road, especially when you consistently put money away and let it grow.

CASE STUDY: ADVICE FROM A FINANCIAL EXPERT

Andrew Housser — Co-CEO of Bills.com

Get creative with saving!

Sell unneeded items on eBay, hold a yard sale, or put change into a jar every evening and save the proceeds when you cash it in. Even small amounts, when saved regularly, will accumulate surprisingly quickly.

Give up expensive coffee drinks. If you hit Starbucks twice a week, break the habit for eight weeks and save $64. To make the habit permanent, spend $10 on an insulated container and bring coffee made from home. Short-term savings: $50 if you spring for the container. Long-term savings if you bank the money saved and thank compound interest: $136,000 over 25-30 years.

Drive less. Walk, bike, or carpool. Drive your car about 25 miles less a week and you'll have saved another $68,000 over 25-30 years (depending on type of car, mileage, and cost of fuel).

Eat out less. Make lunch or dinner at home instead of "grabbing a quick bite." Saving $10, $20, or more each week by cutting out a restaurant meal or two adds up to hundreds in a few months.

Spend with cash. People who do not use debit cards or credit cards are less likely to throw that extra item into the shopping cart. You'll be pleasantly surprised at the end of the month.

Redeem credit card rewards. If you're an older teen or college student with a credit card, check your credit card statements to see how many rewards "points" you have. Then, visit the rewards website to find out if you can convert the rewards into cash or gift cards. Some credit cards even double the value of your rewards at specific retailers.

They All Want Your Money

$ave $mart Tip

Check out a savings calculator online that estimates compound interest to see how much you can save over a long period of time:

www.math.com/students/calculators/source/compound.htm

How many times have you seen a magazine ad or a television commercial where the teens within the advertisement seemed really cheesy? You probably laughed at the marketer's attempt at appealing to teenagers because it was so far off the mark. The teens in the ad were wearing clothes that no one really wears, dancing to music that no one really listens to. All in all, the ad was incredibly fake and made you wonder why marketers try so hard to get your attention.

As a teen, you are within a group that is highly valuable and intriguing to advertisers. You have what is referred to as disposable income, which means you have money you can spend without worrying you won't be able to pay your mortgage payment or put food on the table. Advertisers want to figure out how to get you to spend, spend, spend, and they don't want you to know they're trying so hard.

If you are going to take control of your money and your spending, you need to know marketers are always throwing messages at you, even when you don't realize it's happening. What types of messages are they throwing at you? They want you to feel as though you need their product in order to be popular, or that their product will make your life better than it is now. They use many different types of advertising to influence you to buy certain clothes, listen to certain types of music, and eat certain types of food. While you can easily spot a bad attempt at getting you to buy something (think about the last cheesy advertisement you saw featuring teenagers or college students), it isn't always easy to spot the better attempts. Not all advertising comes in the form of an ad on TV or in a magazine. Marketers are far sneakier than that. You are probably being assaulted with advertising no matter where you go, whether it's in school, while riding in a car, or just walking down the street with your friends.

Pay attention the next time you go to see a movie in a theater. Right away, you will encounter advertisements for other movies, as well as advertisements for products. Signs and videos playing on screens overhead will try to urge you to buy one snack over another at the snack counter. The people who sell you popcorn may wear buttons advertising certain drinks. And the advertisement assault doesn't end when the movie begins. If you make a conscious effort to catch all the advertisements snuck into the movie (also called product placement), you will realize marketers never really stop with their attempt to get teenagers to spend money. Companies pay big bucks to have their products featured in movies. They know a certain car driven by a celebrity during an action movie or a jacket worn by a leading lady in a romance may influence viewers to also buy these items. The scary thing is most people don't even realize these thoughts are entering their minds; they know they want a certain product, but don't really stop to think about where the desire first came from.

Find Out More

Check out the PBS documentary *The Merchants of Cool* to learn more about how marketers try to understand and influence teen spending at **www.pbs.org/wgbh/pages/frontline/shows/cool**.

Why do you need to know this? You now know that one of the best way to take control of your money is to first control your spending. You should realize companies depend on your being unable to resist the urge to buy things you don't need. Right now, there are many well-paid executives sitting in a fancy boardroom trying to figure out exactly how to get you and your money to part ways. They pay teenagers to tell them what is cool and what isn't; they send professionals undercover to blend in with college students to find out the latest fads; and they use this research to develop marketing campaigns designed to get your attention. Wouldn't you rather decide on your own what you want to buy, instead of having someone else tell you what you want? Once you are able to spot advertisements intended to make you spend money on things you don't need, you will be more likely to spend money consciously, and it will become easier to resist their spell.

Impulse buying

How many times have you bought something on impulse? You know you're making an impulse purchase when you buy something you had no intention of buying and you later realize it wasn't even something you needed. Maybe you see a shirt in a store window and impulsively decide to buy it, but by the time you get the shirt home, you realize that you don't even really like it and will probably never wear it, so the shirt just sits in your closet without ever being worn. Sometimes people buy things on impulse because they can't find exactly what their looking for, they're bored, their friends are making purchases, or they don't want to leave the store without buying something.

Impulse buying can turn into a larger problem when it evolves into compulsive shopping. Compulsive shoppers buy items because they can't resist the urge to shop. They also usually claim to feel a "rush" or a "high" from shopping, which is quickly replaced with feelings of guilt or depression. This is considered an addiction by some behavioral scientists, just like a drug addiction or a gambling addiction. Compulsive shoppers usually hide purchases from friends and family and commonly fall deeply into debt — with debt sometimes reaching hundreds of thousands of dollars — before they ever seek help. It's not normal to get a huge rush out of making purchases at a store, and it isn't normal to feel anxious when you are not shopping. If this sounds like something you have experienced, get some help. Talk to your parents, a guidance counselor at your school, or go online and look for local resources such as a Shopaholics Anonymous (**www.shopaholicsanonymous.org**) group — yes, they really do exist.

Chances are, however, you don't fall into the category of a compulsive shopper, but instead, do have some experience with impulse buying. While it may be fun to buy something without having planned it out beforehand, too many instances of impulse buying will drain your wallet and may lead to more serious problems in the future.

Here are some tips to avoid impulse buying:

- **Think through your purchases before you make them**. You are going to run out of money quickly if you make purchases without first considering how the purchase will impact your finances. This doesn't mean you have to mull over buying a cookie for 20 minutes, but it does mean that you shouldn't make purchases you weren't expecting to make that will have more of an impact on your wallet, such as a $29 shirt or DVDs that total $40.

- **Leave your credit or debit card at home when you shop**. You might prefer to use a debit card, but if you only take the exact amount of cash needed to make a purchase, it will be impossible to impulsively buy a bunch of other stuff you don't need. That is, of course, unless you have friends with you who are willing to let you borrow money. Don't let this happen. Impulse buying combined with being in debt to your friends equals trouble. You run the risk of not only falling deeply into debt, but also losing some friends when you don't pay them back.

- **Budget your spending**. If you have a written budget — and stick to it — you will be much less likely to make impulse purchases. *You will learn more about budgeting your money and tracking your spending in Chapter 4.*

Everyone makes impulse purchases once in a while. If you slip up and buy something you were not planning on to buy, don't beat yourself up over it. Accept it as a learning experience and move on.

Sure, you can spend

You don't have to plop every cent you get into a savings account and never touch it. Money should be enjoyed, as long as that enjoyment is combined with some saving too. If you can find a balance between saving and spending, you will have an easier time with your finances than most other people do, while also having the ability to buy the things you want without draining your savings account. The trick is to figure out how to save money on all the things you want most. In the following sections, you will find strategies for saving money while you spend it.

In order to make money, stores purchase merchandise at a low cost, then charge customers a much larger price for the same merchandise. Doing so allows the company to not only make back the money they spent to purchase the products, but to make additional money as well — this is referred to as making a **profit**. Take, for example, for a $25 backpack you purchase in August before heading back to school. You feel good about the purchase because even though you didn't buy the cheapest backpack in the store, you didn't buy the most expensive backpack, either.

After school has been in session for three or four weeks, you see the very same backpack you bought for $25 sitting on the clearance rack for $19. Not all of the backpacks have sold over the next few days, so soon you spy the same backpacks for $12. Then, the price drops to $8.50. One lone backpack won't sell, so the retailer slashes the price down to $4.99 in an attempt to clear out the last of the school supplies and make room for Halloween merchandise. So, the backpack you bought for $25 is now available for less than five dollars, just because a few weeks have passed and the store wants to sell the merchandise.

$ave $mart Tip

Buy school supplies in mid to late September, after all the schools have started their sessions.

How can stores afford to slash prices like this? Stores — especially large retailers — have the buying power to buy items in bulk for reduced prices. There is no way the retailer spent $25 when it originally bought the backpack you purchased, or even close to

$25. In fact, chances are the retailer spent a lot closer to the clearance price for the backpack instead of the full amount you paid.

This is how stores can afford to offer discounts and have sales. They would rather charge you less for an item than send it back to the supplier. This is also why it isn't unreasonable to expect you should be able buy something for less than for the original price. You can expect just about everything will go on sale at some point, even if it is a hot new item that everyone wants. If you wait to buy something until it has been marked down substantially, you're not only saving money, but you're beating the store at its own game.

It isn't always easy to wait for things to go on sale or wait to get your hands on a coupon so you can buy something at a reduced cost. It sure beats seeing something on a clearance rack priced at a fraction of what you paid for it, though. If you can figure out how to buy in the "off-season," you can save yourself a bunch of money. Using the example of the backpack, the best (and cheapest) time to buy school supplies is *after* school starts because stores want to get rid of all the extra school supplies they have lining the shelves. If you can remember to buy what you need the year before, such as buying notebooks and pens this year when school supplies go on sale because you know you will also need them next year, you will save quite a bit of money. Otherwise, you can at least remember to load up on all the school supplies you will need for the remainder of the school year — and snatch up any extras you might like, such as art supplies — when all the school supplies go on clearance.

The same goes for clothes. The best time to buy summer clothes is at the end of the season, when stores are trying to make room for their autumn clothes. Retailers get anxious to clear the store of seasonal clothing when the season is nearing its end because they don't want to take a financial loss on the clothes that haven't been purchased by customers yet, so this is the time to buy new clothes. The good news for you is many retailers are restless with seasonal stock, so bathing suits might go on clearance racks in July, or you might be able to score a great winter coat on clearance while there is still snow on the ground. Retailers can be a little funny when it comes to this stuff, so pay attention to how your favorite stores rotate their stock. You will begin to notice a real trend that is actually easy to follow, and you will know when you should buy something or when should wait for them to wind up on sale. If you talk to an employee who works at your favorite store, you might be able to find out when things go on sale and the lowest cost you can expect to pay.

Shop around

Did you know: Different stores charge different amounts for the same products? You might pay $16 for a shirt in one store, but $12 for the same shirt at another store on the other side of town. The truth is, some stores charge more for a variety of reasons. These stores might offer excellent customer service, so they feel they can charge more for their items. They might also believe the area of town they are located in justifies higher prices, such as stores located in a wealthy part of town. Whatever the reasoning, you should be aware the price you find at one store is not necessarily the same price you will find everywhere else. The trick is to figure out which store offers the item you need to buy at the cheapest price. Keep in mind that just because a particular store advertises itself as having the lowest prices does not mean this is 100 percent true all the time.

Suppose you want to buy a video game. The store closest to you — and the one you usually shop at — has the game for $59. You find the game advertised at a store across town for $49. Don't pay the $59! You should either find a way to get to the store across town or take the ad from the other store to your local store. Show the ad to the manager at the store and tell him or her you want the same price. This store wants your business — and your money. There is a good chance you will get the game for $49. Some stores call this a "best price guarantee" or something similar, but it's a common practice that can save you a lot of money if you pay attention to how much various stores charge for the items you want to buy. You can compare prices online or by sifting through ads in newspapers and magazines.

Renting versus buying

Who says you have to *buy* everything that you want? If you are looking to read a certain book or watch a certain movie, you may not even have to buy the item. Instead, you might want to think about a few other options you have that cost a lot less, or might not even cost any money at all:

- **Rental services**: Services like Netflix (**www.netflix.com**), Gamefly (**www.gamefly.com**), or Booksfree.com (**www.booksfree.com**) require a small monthly fee, but allow you to borrow games, books, and movies for an extended period of time. You return the game or movie via mail when you are done with it and another from your list arrives at your home. Some rental services also allow you access to movies online, so you don't even have to wait for the movie to come in the mail. How much you pay each month for these services depends on which membership plan you sign up for. Keep in mind: You will need to have a parent's permission to sign up if you are under 18. You will also need a credit card or checking account to pay for your membership unless someone gives you a gift membership.

- **Free services**: You local library is one of the best places to find books, movies, magazines, and more. Usually the only fees you will ever have to pay are late fees if you return items after the due date. Also, if you live outside of city limits, you may have to pay a small annual fee for the use of the library. Even with these fees, this can still be one of the cheapest ways to get your hands on some things you would have to pay for otherwise.

$ave $mart Tip

If you have a favorite store where you usually spend the majority of your money, you may want to consider this store when the time comes to get a part-time job. Most stores offer employee discounts that can save you a lot of money. You will learn more about getting a job in Chapter 8.

Obviously, you aren't going to stop shopping altogether. However, there is no reason why you shouldn't save some money while you're at it. Once you realize that you don't have to pay full price for things, you will also quickly notice that your money lasts a lot longer than it used to.

Secondhand stores (also called consignment stores or thrift stores) can sometimes have the best merchandise at the lowest prices. Not only can you find books, movies, and games in these stores, but you can also find clothes, musical instruments, room décor, and all sorts of interesting things. Sometimes, the condition of these items might be a little rocky, but every once in a while, you will come across something that is nearly brand new. That's the fun part about buying things secondhand; it's like a treasure hunt. You can also buy used items online, and sometimes, this is the best way to get your hands on the things you want without paying full price. Consignment shops aren't usually in the mall. To find one near you, search online or look in your telephone directory.

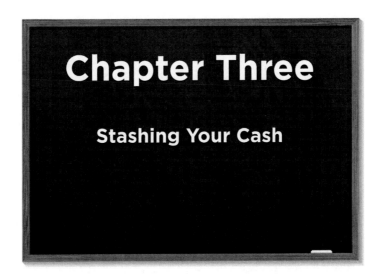

Chapter Three

Stashing Your Cash

You might already have a bank account you maintain well. If so, that's great! There are many people who get far into adulthood and never really figure out how to manage their bank accounts, so you're already ahead of the game.

Why don't some people maintain their bank accounts well? A lot of people were never taught how to effectively manage a bank account, and other people get scared because there are numbers involved. Don't worry; not only will you learn everything you need to know about maintaining a bank account in this chapter, but you will also learn that the numbers involved in money are nothing to be afraid of. There is nothing you will ever do with your bank accounts that can't be done with simple math using a calculator.

Bank accounts aren't complicated at all. In fact, once you learn everything you need to know, you might wonder what all the fuss is about.

Did You Know?

"[When searching for a bank], start with your parents' credit union. They often offer the best deals and are more accommodating to their members than larger commercial banks."

Christopher Lawson, private wealth advisor

Different Types of Bank Accounts

Although there are many different types of accounts, the main focus of this section will be the two accounts you are most likely to encounter as a teenager: savings and checking accounts.

Savings accounts

Savings accounts are meant to be a place to keep money you don't need right away. Some people use savings accounts as a way to save for a specific expense, like a car or a vacation, and some people use them as rainy day or emergency funds. People put money into saving in order to have funds available immediately should the need arise, whatever that need should be. Your parents might have a savings account and probably call it the family savings or something similar.

Many parents open savings accounts for their children when the kids are very young, sometimes right after a baby is born. In the past, if you received a check as a gift and your parent took you to the bank to deposit it, there is a good chance you already have a savings account. There is also a good chance at least one of your parents is listed on the account, so both you and your parents have access to the money in the account until you are old enough to have your own account. Ask your parents if there is already a savings account open in your name, and if so, ask them to show you how much money you have sitting in the account.

Savings accounts pay interest. This is the amount of money the bank pays you, based on how much money you have sitting in the account. Interest is an important personal finance concept you need to learn. You may have heard the term thrown around by your parents with regard to interest paid on credit cards or loans, but in this instance, it is interest paid *by* the financial institution, not *to* the financial institution. When it comes to savings accounts, interest is a good thing. You want to earn as much interest as possible when your money is sitting in a savings account. Banks pay their customers interest because they use the money you deposit to make loans, investments, and other transactions in order to make a profit. Basically, you are loaning the bank money to operate — and they are paying you for letting them use your money.

Here is how a savings account works. You deposit money into your savings account. After you deposit the money, the bank uses it for to perform daily functions and pays you a small amount of money each month —called interest — for letting them use your money. When you are ready to spend your money, you withdraw it from the bank, including any interest that has been paid to your account. The interest you are paid is not usually a lot of money, and the percentage you are paid depends on the current economic climate. When interest rates are low, you may only have a 1 percent interest rate on the money in your savings account, but when interest rates are high, you will be paid a larger percentage. Either way, after a while, the interest you earn can really add up. If you mention the term "compound interest" to someone who has even a small amount of financial knowledge, his or her eyes will probably light up. Here is why:

Compound interest is the term used to explain what happens when interest is added to your account, and you then earn interest on that interest. For example, suppose one month you earn $.05 on a savings account containing $300. You do not add any more money to the account in the next month, but the $.05 is added to your balance and so the next statement shows that your balance is $300.05, plus whatever interest you earn for that month. The amount of interest you earn will keep going up as your balance increases, even if you do not deposit any additional money into your account.

There are complicated formulas and equation for determining compound interest, but what you should be concerned with is that you are making a profit on the money you deposit, even though you aren't actively doing anything with it. Why do banks offer interest payments on savings accounts? There are a couple of reasons, but it basically boils down to banks needing to grow their customer base (and the amount of money customers deposit) in order to perform the main functions of the bank. Banks use the money people deposit to lend money and to make investments. The more customers they have, the more money they will have access to. Think of interest payments as a way of the bank thanking you for letting them play with your money.

The more money you put into your savings account, the more interest you will earn. The longer your money sits in the savings account, the more compound interest can build up. If you don't already have a savings account, talk to your parents about helping you open one. Keep these things in mind:

- Look for a fee-free savings account. Most banks offer special savings accounts for students that have no minimum balance requirement and don't have many, if any, fees. You will learn more about the fees you may encounter at your bank later in this chapter. Make sure this is the type of account you open, because some bank tellers might try to steer you toward a different type of account that has fees.

- One of your parents will probably have to be on the account until you are 18. This means your parent will be able to take a look at your account  any time and may even be able to withdraw money at any time, and you may need a parent's signature to withdraw any money from the account. You should check with your bank to determine the different types of savings accounts they offer, and which is best for you. Most financial institutions have more than one type, so look for the simplest account designed specifically for minors or college students. There are plenty of advantages to these types of accounts designed specifically for minors. Often, they do not have the same fees and regulations that the savings accounts designed for adults may have. For example, a traditional savings account may have a minimum balance requirement, which means that the account holder must keep a certain amount of money in the account otherwise a monthly fee is charged. Savings accounts designed for minors usually don't have this feature, and if they do, you need to find a different financial institution. *You will learn about choosing a financial institution later in this chapter. You will also learn about making deposits and withdrawals once you do get an account.*

Checking accounts

You may not need a checking account right now, but once you have a steady income and recurring bills to pay, you will definitely want to open an account like this. A checking account allows you easier access to your money because you can write checks from the account, and you may even have a check card issued to you.

Checks are basically paper promises of money. You write a check from your account and give the check to a person or store, who then turns around and demands the money from your bank. This money is debited from your account. Check cards look like credit cards and feature a Visa or MasterCard logo, but they aren't actually credit cards. Instead, you use the card to make a purchase, and the money is immediately withdrawn from your checking account. These cards are also commonly called debit cards. The next chapter will cover check cards in more detail.

Do you need a checking account? If you have money going in and out of your account often, such as when you get a weekly paycheck, and you have recurring bills to pay, this is a good account to have. This is especially true if you need an easy way to pay bills or to access your money, as savings accounts often feature restrictions on how often you can withdraw money. Just like the savings account, you should be able to find a checking account that is specifically designed for teens. You will probably be required to have one of your parents listed on the account with you until you are over 18 years of age, but check with your bank to find out what options you have.

You don't need a checking account if you just need somewhere to put money you get once in a while, such as birthdays and holidays. A checking account is a good idea if you have a job and a steady income, but if you just need an account for the occasional checks you get from family for birthdays and other special occasions, stick to a savings account for now.

Here is a quick glance at some of the differences and similarities between checking and savings accounts.

Checking Account	Savings Account
Easy access to cash with checks and debit cards.	Access to cash through an ATM is sometimes offered.
Interest may be paid, but is usually low.	Higher interest is earned with savings accounts.
This account can be used to pay bills online or over the phone.	There may be restrictions regarding electronic payments from this account.

CASE STUDY: BUDGETING AN ALLOWANCE

Jasmine Richardson – High School Student

My personal finance is based around the money my parents give me. As a sophomore, I am learning how to set budgets and build my own savings. On average, my parents give me about $15 a week for lunch. I have to manage how much money I spend each day. Sometimes that requires shifting a few dollars from lunch to other things.

For example, Otis Spunkmeyer cookies are sold for a dollar every Tuesday and Thursday for the schools' special needs program. I have to decide whether I want to buy a cookie or save my money for lunch. Lunch costs $1.75, so if I only have $2 in my pocket, I will not buy a cookie. This helps me prepare for budgeting my finances when I get a job or go off to college. Also, I am learning how to build my savings. I have certain plans for the future, such as attending a major university, that require a substantial amount of money.

Building my savings account now will help relieve my parents of some of the financial burdens they will face as I enter college. Also, my friend and I are planning to have a combined birthday party when we turn 18. Because graduation day is close to that, we were considering starting a savings account specifically for the party. This will help me learn how to create and control my savings in the future. It is safe to say I have learned from personal experience how to set budgets and build savings. At such a young age, I still have a lot of learning left to do.

Other types of accounts

Most of the accounts offered at financial institutions are a form of a savings or checking account. Here is a brief list of some of the other accounts commonly offered by banks, and the instances when you might have a reason, as a teenager or college student, to open one of these accounts:

- **Money market accounts**: This is a savings account that pays a higher interest rate than a regular savings account. A money market account may also allow account holders to access the funds in the account using a checkbook issued from the account. There is usually a higher minimum balance required to open a money market account (generally $500-$1,000) and more restrictions regarding how many withdrawals you can make before fees are charged.

  When would a money market account be a good idea for a teenager or college student? If you have a substantial amount of money (a few thousand dollars, for instance) you want to put into an account to earn interest, and you don't plan on taking the money out any time soon, a money market account may be a good idea. For example, suppose your grandfather sends everyone in the family $3,000 each as a gift, but you aren't quite sure what you want to do with your $3,000 yet. You can put it into a money market account to earn interest while you figure out how you would like to spend the money. Talk to a bank representative to find out about the minimum opening deposit and other possible restrictions.

- **Certificates of deposits (CDs)**: A certificate of deposit is a savings account that pays high interest, but you aren't allowed to withdraw your money for a certain period of time. Most banks offer a variety of timelines for CDs. For example, you can open a 6-month CD, which requires you to keep the money in the account for 6 months and to not take any of the money out. In return, the bank gives you a high interest rate, which means you make money out of the arrangement. The longer you keep the money in the CD, the more money you will make.

When would a CD be a good idea for a teenager or college student? If you have a large sum of money you want to put away for a certain amount of time — such as if a relative gives you $1,000 for a **down payment** on a car you want to buy next year — then a CD can be a great place to put the money. Not only will you earn a lot of interest on the money, but you also won't be tempted to spend it because you won't be allowed access to the funds until the specified period of time is up.

- **Mutual fund accounts**: Mutual funds are a form of investing that can involve a lot less risk than investing in individual stocks. Many banks offer mutual fund accounts where investment money is pooled by a group of people instead of one person alone. This is a type of savings account that can earn a lot of interest — but you can also lose all the money you deposit if the funds don't do well.

  When would a mutual fund account be a good idea for a teenager or college student? If you already have another savings account in place, and you are ready to try your hands at investing, this can be a great way to start. You shouldn't put money in a mutual fund account that you can't afford to lose, though, so this isn't the best place to put money you have earmarked for something else in the future. Talk to a representative at your bank about the fees that may be involved with this type of account before you sign up.

Financial institutions offer plenty of other accounts that are credit products, such as credit cards and loans.

Putting Money into Your Savings or Checking Account

Banks try to make depositing money as easy as possible. You can visit the bank and make your deposit with a customer service representative, often referred to as a teller. The teller will tally up the total amount of your deposit, including cash, checks, and money orders, and give you a receipt. Insist on a receipt. Not only does it prove you actually made the deposit, but it will help you to remember how much you put into your account when you record the deposit in your savings account register, software program, or any other method you use to keep track of the money in your account. You can also add money to your accounting by making your deposit with an automatic teller machine (ATM).

Did You Know?

Interest rates constantly change according to what is going on in the financial world. Even if you open a savings account with a certain interest rate, it can drop lower or climb higher at any time.

Depositing money by mail

If you don't want to, or can't, physically go to the bank (for example, military dependents living overseas) to make the deposit, you have a few other choices. It is possible to mail checks or money orders — but not cash — into the bank, but be sure you do a few things first:

1. Completely fill out your deposit slip. Deposit slips vary from one bank to another, but filling them out is usually as easy as following the printed instructions. Your bank will give you deposit slips with your name and account information printed on them when you open the account, either in a separate book or in the back of your checkbook. If you don't have either of these, you can use one of the blank deposit slips provided at the bank. If you know you will be unable to visit your bank for an extended period of time, pick up a few blank deposit slips when you can. If you don't have access to any of these forms, and you need to make a deposit immediately, you can create your own deposit slip worded like this:

Please place this deposit total of (amount) into my account (account number).

Itemize the deposits if there is more than one check or money order. For example, if you send two checks, detail them on the letter like this:

Check #2241: $25, Check #101: $110, Total Deposit: $135

Date the form, make sure it can be read, sign the bottom, and double-check to make sure all the information is correct before you drop the deposit in the mail.

You now need to endorse the check. Your signature on the check allows the bank access to the funds from the deposit in order to place them into your account. If you do not sign the checks, the bank may not accept the deposit. Write your account number directly beneath your signature. This helps the teller who receives your deposit to credit the deposit to the correct account, especially if your checks get separated from your deposit slip for one reason or another. Flip your check over and sign it. Most checks have a line indicating to "endorse here." On the opposite side of the check, you will see a notice that warns you this area is for financial institution use only — do not sign in this area. This is the spot where the bank stamps the check for record-keeping when it has been accepted and deposited.

Sign the back of the checks or money orders with the same name you used to open your account. If your legal first name is Zachary, and this is how you opened the account, — but all your friends know you are Zach — you should still sign the checks with Zachary.

2. You can also choose to write "For Deposit Only" on the back of the checks instead of using your signature. You cannot sign the back of the checks or money orders using "For Deposit Only" if you are taking them into the bank and want to get cash back from the deposit instead of depositing the full amount.

3. Place the deposit slip and the checks and/or money orders into an envelope. If your bank supplies you with envelopes, use this envelope. Chances are, though, you will have to supply your own envelope. There are a few very important details to keep in mind when selecting an envelope to make a deposit to any bank account:

- **Make sure you have the address right.** Some financial institutions have more than one address and may have a specific address for deposits. In fact, if your account is with a large financial institution, you may not be allowed to just mail your deposit to your local branch. You may instead have to send it to a large processing center at a different address; otherwise, there might be a delay in getting the funds into your account. It's not fun to have money delayed when you are waiting for it, but if you don't send the deposit to the correct address, it may not show up in your account as soon as you would like.

- **Make sure your return address is on the envelope.** If you forget a stamp or don't put the correct address for the bank on the envelope, the post office won't know whom to send the envelope back to. Imagine your deposit sitting somewhere in a bin at the post office because they can't figure out where to send it to. You will probably lose your deposit if this happens.

- **Choose an envelope that isn't see-through.** Like it or not, sometimes mail gets stolen. Using a see-through envelope puts your money at risk for being stolen. For someone looking to steal bank deposits, it will be obvious there are checks or money orders contained within. Instead, use an envelope that is specifically designed for mail like this. These envelopes have markings on the inside of the envelope that makes it virtually impossible to know what it inside without actually opening the envelope.

These may seem like a lot of instructions, but once you have been through the process once or twice, it becomes really simple. The point is to make sure you include all the information necessary for the bank to deposit your money into your account without a delay, while also making sure your deposit doesn't get lost on the way to the bank.

Depositing money by ATM

You can also make deposits using an ATM if your bank has issued you an ATM card (which includes check cards, debit cards, and ATM cards that can only be used at ATMs). This is a quick and easy way to make a deposit as long as you follow the directions on the ATM screen. You will need to have an ATM card, and you must know the Personal Identification Number (PIN) for the card in order to make a deposit.

 ### *Safety First!*

Your PIN might be assigned to you by your bank when you open your account, or you may be able to choose a PIN yourself. Either way, **never** share your PIN with your friends, and **don't** write your PIN on your ATM card. Memorize the number instead. If someone else learns your PIN, your account can easily get hacked into, and your money may get stolen.

Use an ATM belonging to your financial institution when trying to make a deposit. You will know which institution the ATM belongs to by looking at the signs on the ATM. For example, if you have an account with Bank of America, do not attempt to make a deposit at a Wells Fargo ATM. Making a deposit into your savings or checking account using an ATM is usually as easy as following the prompts on the screen, but the process usually follows the same format each time.

1. Insert your card into the ATM. There will typically be an image of an ATM card showing you the proper format for inserting the card. The screen will then ask you for your PIN, which you will enter using the keypad. The keypad may appear as a touch screen on the actual screen of the ATM. Make sure no one is standing nearby trying to get a peek at your PIN number. If you notice anyone nearby who

seems like he or she may have criminal intentions, cancel the transaction, retrieve your card, and walk away. It's better to be safe than sorry. You should also pay attention to your surroundings. Don't use an ATM that isn't well-lit or that seems deserted. Take extra precautions when using an ATM at night. A good rule of thumb is to avoid ATMs in locations where you feel uncomfortable.

2. After you input your PIN, the ATM screen will ask you what you want to do next. Look at the menu on the screen to find the button that says "Make a Deposit" or something similar. At this point, you should already have your deposit form filled out, your checks signed, and all of these documents should be in an envelope. You will find the proper envelope in a drawer near or on the ATM, or you can get these envelopes inside the bank. Keep in mind: Some banks don't require deposit slips or deposit envelopes for ATM deposits. With some banks, you can insert your check or cash directly into ATM without needing an envelope. Ask a bank representative for details on whether this is the case at your bank.

3. If you have more than one account — such as a savings and a checking account — the ATM screen will ask you to specify which account you want the money to go into. Hit the button for whichever account you wish to deposit your money into. The screen may ask you to verify your intentions at certain points, so if the information is correct, just hit the button to proceed.

4. The ATM screen will probably ask you at this point to input the amount of your deposit. Using the keypad, type in the exact amount of your deposit. If you are depositing more than one check or money order, input the total amount. Most ATMs accept the deposit amount in dollars and cents, so if your deposit totals one hundred dollars, input it with the decimals (100.00, not 100); otherwise, the ATM may only credit you for a dollar deposit because of the missing decimal. Don't lie about the amount you are depositing. If you purposely enter an incorrect amount, you'll wind up being charged large fees and the bank may close your account.

5. Once you have entered all your information, the ATM will ask you to insert the envelope. Most ATMs have a slot that opens up when you make an envelope deposit, so look for directions showing you how to correctly insert the envelope. The screen will then ask you if you want a receipt, to which you should reply "yes." Keep the printed receipt until you know for sure the correct amount has been credited to your account.

Making an ATM deposit is actually a lot easier than it sounds. It's as easy as following the prompts on the screen, and if you ever get confused or lost with the directions presented on the screen you can always hit the "back" button or cancel the transaction altogether and start again. Because the process for making an ATM deposit will vary from one bank to another, ask a bank representative to walk you through the process the first time to avoid mistakes.

Depositing money by other means

You can also make deposits into your account using direct deposit, which allows your employer to electronically deliver a paycheck into your account without issuing a paper check or handing you cash. Not all businesses offer direct deposit, so check with your employer to find out if they do.

Some banks allow you to make deposits in other ways. You may be able to scan a check and send the image to the bank via e-mail, and they will credit the amount to your account that way. They can do this because all the information they need is listed on the face of the check. Once you make the deposit, the check is no longer valid, and you should shred the original check because the money has been electronically withdrawn from and deposited into your account. Some financial institutions will even allow you to take a picture of the check with your cell phone, send them the image, and deposit it that way. As this technology advances, more banks will offer this type of deposit feature, but USAA (**www.usaa.com**) is one of the first financial institutions to offer this feature. Different financial institutions have different depositing rules, so check with your bank to find out the different options available for making deposits.

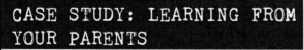

CASE STUDY: LEARNING FROM YOUR PARENTS

Kate — High School Student

From the beginning, my parents taught me to save my money — and when I have to spend it, to spend it responsibly. With a few exceptions, I have stuck to this advice for most of my life, and it has been a benefit to me on numerous occasions.

Saving rather than spending most of my money is especially important for me because I don't have a job; it's not possible with my schoolwork, community service activities, and chores at home. As a result, I halve all of the money I receive as gifts for my birthday and Christmas. Half of this money goes into a savings account, and I take the other half as spending money. This system has actually worked great for me. I have built up a considerable sum in my savings account. Currently, this money is helping to pay my car insurance bill, and come next year, I will be putting most of it toward various college expenses. Though the Florida Bright Futures Scholarship Program will be paying for my tuition, there is still housing, food, a laptop, and books to pay for. In this way, saving my money has really been worth it.

I have also reaped the benefits of managing my spending money well. Whenever my parents pay me for doing a chore — cleaning the house, etc. — I put half of the money in my wallet and half into a jar. Obviously, I spend the money in my wallet quickly, but I save the money in the jar for big expenditures like concert tickets and new electronics. I have had a lot of success doing this; it prevents me from spending all of my money immediately, as well as having to borrow money from my parents.

Saving money is definitely one of those habits you need to get into as a teenager. I feel that since I have thus far managed my finances well, I am prepared for the various monetary difficulties that I am bound to face in college and beyond.

Where Should You Put Your Money?

Now that you know the accounts offered at financial institutions, you might be wondering where exactly you should put your money. You may have friends who simply stuff their money into a jar and hide the jar in their bedroom, and you may have friends who have more than one bank account. How do you know which option is best for you?

If you do not have a bank account right now, don't panic. You do not have to run out and open a savings account and a check-

ing account, and feverishly research the best mutual fund account. This is something you can take one step at a time and not feel rushed.

The account best suited for you has a lot to do with your money situation at this point. Which of the following scenarios sounds like you?

1. **You don't have a steady income, like a job or an allowance.** If this is the case, open a simple student savings account that does not have a minimum balance or minimum monthly deposit requirement. Use the account to put some money away whenever you have the opportunity.

2. **You get large chunks of money as gifts or from doing work once in a while, such as babysitting or mowing lawns, but you don't have a recurring income**. A simple savings account is a good idea for you, unless the chunks of money you get are very substantial and you plan on putting most or all of the money away. If this is the case, look at a money market account. If you plan on withdrawing money from the account a lot, consider a simple savings account or a checking account, but be sure to get a student checking account so you won't get fees for not having direct deposit.

3. **You have a job and get paid on a regular basis**. A savings account may be sufficient for you unless you need access to your money regularly, in which case a checking account may be the best place to put your money. As with the scenario above, make sure the checking account won't charge

a fee for a low balance, or if you do not have direct deposit from your employer.

It is a great idea to have a savings account, even if you do not have a lot of money to put into it right now. A savings account allows you start learning about putting money aside, and additionally, you won't have to scramble to open a bank account when you do land a job and your employer wants to set you up on direct deposit.

Another advantage to opening a savings account at an early age is that it gives you a history with the bank. In the future, when you want to get a loan (for a car or a house), your bank may be more willing to lend you money because of your long history as an account holder in good standing. Besides, maybe just having a savings account will prompt you to want to start putting money into the account.

If you already have a bank account, but aren't sure how much money is in it or how the account works, it is time to get this all figured out. It may be that the account you have isn't the best account for you; your account may have high monthly fees that are erasing your balance. It is completely legal for a bank to fee your account every month as long as you were notified of the fees at one time. For example, suppose you opened an account and did not read the paperwork the bank representative gave to you. Within that paperwork, it may have stated if you don't have at least $200 in your bank account at all times, you will receive a $10 fee each month. Before you know it, your entire balance is down to zero because of the fees, and then the bank starts charging you additional fees because of your negative balance.

Sounds deceitful, doesn't it? Always keep in mind: Financial institutions need to make money, and these fees are one of the ways they do it. This is why it is important to know what is going on with your account, especially if you have had it for a long time and never really took the time to read all the paperwork the representative gave you when you first opened the account. If you do not have access to the original paperwork, check with the bank's website. Sometimes, this information will be featured online. Otherwise, contact a representative at your financial institution to have the terms of your bank account fully explained to you. If there is something you do not understand, ask more questions. Remember: Your bank works *for you*.

CASE STUDY: WHAT HAPPENS NEXT?

Meaghan – High School Student

I am definitely the type of teenager who will be in for a rude awakening when I go to college and have to deal with my own finances. I have only ever had one real job – a summer job at my father's medical office. I have never filled out a job application, filed taxes, managed a bank account, or written a check. I realize that soon my parents will have to teach me all of these things, and I really wish I had been exposed to it earlier.

My parents have always been the money-makers and the ones to deal with money in my house. Neither of my sisters have managed their own finances, either; although they are younger and have more time to learn. I still have an allowance at home that my parents give me weekly, and I guess I could say I have learned to manage that because they do not just dish out more when I run out. I know to save for upcoming holidays and birthdays, and I try not to blow the money I do get in one weekend. But I admit, it is easier said than done. Often, I find myself asking for more money and wonder what will happen next year.

Develop your plan

There is a rule in personal finance called the 10 percent rule. This is a rule many people follow, dictating how much money they put away into a savings account intended for nothing more than emergencies. This is a fund that is not for a specific purchase; instead, it is money that you put away "just in case." But just in case *what*? If you are an adult out on your own, this money is there in case you lose your job and do not have an income, yet still have to pay all your bills until you can find another job. Adults might also use this money if an unexpected expense comes up, such as the car breaking down and needing costly repairs, or medical bills from an illness or injury.

$ave $mart Tip

For young adults living on their own, a sufficient "emergency fund" should have 3-6 months' worth of expenses. That means you should be able to live comfortably for 3-6 months from the money in your emergency fund without any income coming in at all.

This rule says you should always put 10 percent of what you earn into your savings account. It doesn't matter if you make $100 a month or $1,000 a month; as a teenager, you can start building up an impressive amount of money, and by the time you need the money as an adult, you won't have to worry about having to come up with this money once an emergency happens. Don't forget about the concept of compound interest. You may not feel like you are putting away very much money when you only put away 10 percent, but you are setting the stage for interest to accrue, or build up. Before you know it, you will have quite a bit of money stashed away.

You should decide whether you want to open up a savings account that is specific to your 10 percent savings. Some people find that if they keep this money separate from their other money, they are much less likely to spend it. If you put all your money into a checking account with the intention of not touching 10 percent of what you deposit, you will probably soon find that, despite your efforts, all the money gets spent. Keeping the 10 percent separate is a good idea because you won't be tempted to borrow from it for unnecessary expenses.

For this reason, you probably need two bank accounts at this point: a 10 percent savings account and another account, whether it's a checking account or another savings account you access frequently. The savings account should be located in a financial institution where it is easy to make deposits. In other words, if your aunt from out of state is nice enough to open a savings account for you, but the account is located at a bank near her instead of near you, this may not be the best place to put your 10 percent. This would be true unless you can use direct deposit to deposit the 10 percent each time you get paid, or if the bank makes it easy to make deposits with features such as cell phone photo deposits. If it is difficult to make deposits to the bank, this isn't the account that you should use for your emergency fund.

What should the other account be? It depends on your needs and how much money you are dealing with. If you already have a job and a recurring income, a checking account is a good idea. You will have access to your money easily through checks and a debit card. If, on the other hand, you do not have a recurring income — or you don't really need to access your money all that often — a savings account is sufficient. When you hit adulthood, you should absolutely have a checking and a savings account, as well as an additional account for your emergency fund. Why not go ahead and set up these accounts now, since you know you will need them down the road?

Once you have an emergency fund account, a regular savings account, and a checking account, you need to develop your plan for where the money will go. If you are saving for something in particular, like a car or a road trip you want to take with your friends in the near future, you may want to put more money into your regular savings account to get ready for this expense. Otherwise, consider setting up a plan that is something like this:

- Deposit 10 percent of your income into the emergency fund.
- Deposit another 10 percent to 40 percent of your income into the regular savings account.
- Deposit the rest of your income into the checking account.

Have you heard the saying pay yourself first? This phrase means you should always make sure you put money into your savings account before you buy anything unnecessary or spend any money. If you can get into the habit of always paying yourself first, you will develop a really great financial habit that will certainly serve you well when you hit adulthood and have a bunch of bills to pay. Of course, you don't want to avoid paying your bills in order to put money into a savings account, but the goal is to have enough money to save while also paying your bills.

CASE STUDY: SAVING FOR COLLEGE
Shantrell — High School Student

When entering into college for the first time, you may have a lot of things to think about, such as boys, parties, and how exciting it's going to be to live on your own without your parents. But the thing that never really crosses your mind until the last minute is, "How am I going to pay for college?" With college coming up, people sometimes take the easier way out by finding scholarships, by writing essays, getting the necessary paper work, and the hard part — trying to find the time to fill them out. But what if this plan doesn't work out? You always need a backup. There's also the plan of saving your money for things that will benefit your education. Yeah, that's right — *your* own money. I've been saving my money for college for two years now, and I've had some huge results.

My plan, since the time when I got my first job at the age of 16, was to save my money for college and to have at least $1,000 in the bank by the end of the year. And it worked! My mom started my savings account when she first found out I got the job. She set it up with her job so that every two weeks, they would take $15 out of her check to put into my account to get me started. When I received my first paycheck, I took my first $50 out, and from then, on my account flourished. With every check, I began to take out a little bit more at a time until I learned how to handle paying my car insurance, cell phone bill, and other expenses. I even put my whole check in there, too, on some occasions.

I continually keep myself on a budget, consisting of buying things I needed — not wanted. I still treat myself once in awhile, but I only buy things on sale and things I know I can use or wear now and in college. Instead of buying that one pair of shoes to go with that one outfit, or buying that cute shirt that I know I would only wear once, I buy things that will last. Another step I took was clipping coupons — something I never thought I would do.

Furthermore, I looked into asking for money instead of certain gifts for

Christmas, birthdays, and special occasions. Any extra cash I got, even if it's only $5, eventually adds up. The change that just sits in the ashtray in the car all day, ready to be used at some fast food restaurant, could be rolled up and put in a bank to earn interest.

When thinking about college, money is a huge issue. Or it could not be — it just depends on how you set your priorities to make sure you have a bright future.

Picking a bank

Even though all financial institutions are commonly referred to as banks, they do not all fall into this category. A bank is a financial institution that is for-profit, meaning they operate with the sole intention of making money and turning a profit. On the other hand, a credit union is a financial institution that gives every account holder a small portion of ownership into the credit union. This doesn't mean you get to have a desk at the credit union or order employees around, but instead, you get to vote whenever big decisions are made, such as who will run the credit union. Which one should you choose? They both have pros and cons.

A bank may be able to offer lower interest rates than certain credit unions simply because the bank is larger and has more assets. Some banks also have more locations and more ATMs, which may be more convenient for you. Although it varies from one bank to another, banks have notoriously higher fees than most credit unions, and banks generally do not offer the same customer service levels some credit unions do.

Credit unions are usually more focused on the needs of their account holders (who are usually called members instead of customers) and, therefore, may offer better customer service. Because credit unions are more member-centered, you may have an easier time getting a fee reversed or getting a representative to sit down and explain something about your account to you. Credit unions do not accept everyone, however, and you must qualify to become a member based on the membership requirements of the credit union. For example, while some credit unions allow people to join who live in specific areas, others are for groups of employees. For example, people who work for Coca-Cola can join the Coca-Cola Company Family Federal Credit Union®, but people who do not work for this company cannot join unless they have a family member who is a member.

Which financial institution is best for you? Your first consideration should be the convenience of the bank or credit union. You don't have to be concerned so much with the physical location as long as the financial institution offers banking over the phone or over the Internet (often referred to as online banking). You also want to choose a bank or credit union that offers ATMs so you do not have to pay the fees associated with using a different ATM. While it is all right to use another bank's ATM once in a while, know that the other bank will charge you a fee for doing so.

Look for a bank or credit union offering accounts specifically for teenagers. You will save a lot of money by doing so. Opening a regular account will probably cause you to pay a lot of fees overtime, especially if you do not have direct deposit from an employer and do not keep a minimum balance in your account. Because most financial institutions offer teen accounts, you may want to start with the bank or credit union your parents use. If they aren't happy with their financial institution and are always complaining about bad customer service or heavy fees, don't start with the one they use. Instead, ask your friends about where they put their money and if they are happy with their banking experiences.

You can also look around online. There are some banks that are only online and don't have local branches for customers to walk into. Because their operating costs are so much lower, they can afford to pay more interest for savings accounts. You can use a free online comparison tool (like **www.bankrate.com**) to find out which financial institutions have the highest marks in customer satisfaction and the best interest rates. Don't just plop your money into the financial institution closest to your house or school. Make this decision after doing a little research first.

Here are some features you should look for in a financial institution:

- Choose a bank that doesn't charge a lot of fees.
- Choose a bank that offers an account for your needs, such as a student account with no minimum daily balance.
- Choose a bank that offers the features you want, such as online access to your accounts or balance notifications via text message.
- Choose a bank that is close to your house and school.
- Choose a bank that has plenty of ATMs available.

Online Banking

When you set out to find the best financial institution, don't forget to look for a bank with online banking features. Even if you do not use the Internet very much right now, once you start managing your money, you will find that online banking is an incredibly valuable tool. With online banking, you look at your account transactions, see if your deposits have been credited to your account, transfer money from one account to another, pay bills, and even apply for credit products. Why bother standing in line to talk to a representative when you can accomplish what you need to do using the bank's website?

Make sure the financial institution does not charge extra for the use of their online banking features. Some banks and credit unions offer online banking services that can be synchronized with computer budgeting software, which can make managing your money even easier. In fact, if you can do the majority of your banking online, and can manage your spending using a money management software program — such as Microsoft® Money, Quicken, or Moneydance — you will simplify your finances by leaps and bounds.

Fees

You have read a lot about fees, so you might be wondering exactly what fees are charged by financial institutions. You should try to find a bank that does not charge a lot of fees on student accounts. Many people could avoid many of these fees if they used a different bank or opened a different account.

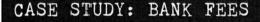

CASE STUDY: BANK FEES

Sandy — Parent

My 16-year-old-son Luke had $100 in his checking account attached to a debit card. In one day, he used his card for a $45 purchase at the mall and a $10 purchase at the movies, leaving him a balance in his checking account of $45. On the way home, he stopped at the gas station, swiped his card at the pump, and put in $25 worth of gas. This should have left him with $20 in his account, but the gas station's machines are pre-set to authorize a hold of $50 when customers pay at the pump. This put his account temporarily into the negative, so when the earlier charges of $45 and $10 posted to his account, he received overdraft fees for both at $29 each.

This is legal and listed in the fine print of the disclosure the bank sent when he received his debit card. It makes more sense to me to make one ATM withdrawal for everything you are going to spend so you don't have issues like these.

It's completely possible to maintain a bank account that is completely fee-less. Find an account that is specifically for teenagers or students that does not charge recurring fees, and make sure to never do anything that might prompt a fee, such as overdrawing your account (writing a check to someone or using your debit card for more money than what you have in your account) or making too many withdrawals on a savings account. These actions will usually cost you money in the form of fees deducted from your bank account balance.

Know what fees your financial institution charges, and avoid fees as much as you can. Do you really want all your money to go to your bank? Instead, keep it in your account.

Here is a list of some of the common fees a bank or credit union may charge. Keep in mind that every financial institution is different, and so are the amounts they will charge. *If you don't find what you're looking for here, additional explanations can be found in the glossary at the end of the book.*

Banking Fee	Description
Abandoned account	This fee may be charged if you have a bank account that has not been used for a certain period of time, usually approximately five years. The bank typically gives the money in the account to the government.
Account maintenance fee	This is a fee charged to your bank account regardless of the type of bank account, nor how much money is in the bank account.
Account closed early	This fee may be charged when the bank researches account discrepancies because there is a problem between the records you have for your bank account and the records that the bank has.
Account research/ reconciliation	This fee may be charged when the bank researches account discrepancies because there is a problem between the records you have for your bank account and the records that the bank has.
ATM	This fee may be charged when you withdraw money from an ATM that does not belong to your bank. This fee ranges anywhere from .50 to around $3. On top of that, you will also be charged a surcharge by the company that owns the ATM.
ATM/debit card replacement	Depending on the bank, you may get one free replacement card if you lose your ATM card. However, if you lose more than one, you will be charged with the cost of replacing the card.
Check printing	This fee may be charged for printing checks for your checking account.
Coin counting	This is generally a free service through most banks, but there is a chance you will be charged for coin counting, especially if you go to a bank to which you are not a member. Coin counting involves bringing in loose change to have the bank count and wrap coins in sleeves.
Counter checks	If you lose your checkbook or need additional checks, you may be charged for counter checks (or temporary checks) given to you by the bank until your new checks have arrived. These usually do not have your name and address imprinted on the top left corner, so you have to fill in your personal information. They are used as a temporary solution until you get your checks. Some merchants will not take counter checks.
Credit reference	This fee may be charged if you are applying for a loan and need the bank to be a credit reference for you.

Debit card	This fee may be charged for every purchase you make on your debit card. This varies depending on the bank.
Deposited item returned (DIR)	When you get a post-dated check, you can deposit it early. However, if that check bounces, you will not only be charged a NSF fee, but also another fee for depositing the check early.
Early-withdrawal fee for CDs	This fee may be charged if you have a Certificate of Deposit (CD) account, and you close it before the date you agreed on with the bank.
Inactive account	This fee may be charged if you do not use your bank account for approximately 90 days. This is usually a quarterly fee that comes into place when you have no withdrawals and no deposits.
Money orders/ cashier's check	Money orders are often used instead of checks, but sometimes a cashier's check will be used. The bank charges you a fee to print money orders or cashier's checks. Cashier's checks usually cost more than a money order.
Monthly service fee	Depending on your bank, this fee may be charged if your account balance goes below a certain amount.
Non-sufficient funds (NSF)	This fee may be charged if you write a check for money you do not have in your account. This is also called bouncing a check.
Notary fees	This fee may be charged when you have a document certified or if you need to have papers notarized by the bank. Certifying or notarizing is a process used when you need to prove that a document came from you.
Overdraft	This fee may be charged if you have overdraft available on your bank account and you overdraw on your account. Overdraft means you don't have enough money in your account to cover a check or debit card purchase, but the bank still allows the transaction. This charge is usually much lower than the charge you are charged for a bounced check, so it is a better alternative in terms of fees.
Return of checks with statement	This fee may be charged if you want your checks sent back to you after they have been canceled.
Safe deposit box	Having a safe deposit box in the bank's vault will cost you a monthly fee.
Stop payment	This fee may be charged if you give out a check and choose to stop payment on it before it is cashed.
Teller fee	There are certain accounts that require you to complete transactions using an automated system, such as online or over the phone. This fee may be charged when you visit the teller for these types of accounts.

If you do wind up being charged a fee you weren't expecting, talk to a representative at your financial institution. Most banks will allow at least one fee refund, but you have to ask first. Suppose you have a checking account and you withdraw money from an ATM of a different bank, but you didn't realize the ATM would charge you $2.50 in addition to the $2 your bank charges you for using the ATM. It is a good idea to call your bank, ask for an explanation of the fees, listen carefully to what is being said to you, and thank the representative for his or her time spent explaining everything to you. Before you hang up, assure the representative you will not make the same mistake again now that you understand how it works, and ask if there is any way you can have the fee reversed. As long as you are polite (and this isn't the second or third time you have attempted this), you may be able to have the charge refunded to your account.

When a fee is "reversed," it means that the bank takes the fee off your account. In the scenario above, the representative would go into your account on his or her computer and refund the $4.50 back to your account. Keep in mind that banks keep records of fee reversals, and many have quotas for how many times fees can be reversed per customer. Ask too many times for fees to be taken off your account and your request will be denied. Also keep in mind: Some financial institutions actually charge a fee for customers to speak to a representative over the phone. If this is the case with your bank, you would be better off walking into the local branch to solve this problem.

One more thing: If the representative says "no" to the fee reversal, and especially if the representative isn't being very nice about it, ask to speak to a manager. You may be a teenager speaking to an adult, but this *does not* give the representative the right to be rude to you or to talk down to you. Remember: These people work for you. Treat them nicely and with respect, but don't allow them to walk all over you.

Chapter Four

Budgeting Basics

Here it is: The chapter that will teach you everything you need to know about budgeting your money. You have probably heard the word budget tossed around a lot, whether it's your parents telling you that a certain expense, "isn't in the family budget," or a newscaster talking grimly about the nation's budget deficit. This chapter will focus on *your* budget. This is where you will really learn how to manage your personal finances and take control of your money.

A budget can be an exciting and powerful thing because it all boils down to your telling your money where to go. You are in charge. Instead of your money coming and going, leaving you broke and wondering where it all went, you will learn to take charge of your finances and figure out where you should spend your money and how much of it you should spend. If you want to be the boss of your money, budgeting is the way to do it.

CASE STUDY: BUDGETING AN ALLOWANCE

Jasmine Richardson – High School Student

Whether a person is going into business or not, financing is needed to pay for everyday needs, and the use of a budget enables one to estimate the cost of items and set aside money to pay for them. I love to play video games, so five years ago, I went video game shopping at an electronics store. As I walked through the aisles, I found what I was looking for. I took my money out of my pocket to pay for it, but when I looked at the price tag, the amount I had was way below the price. I was determined to get it one way or another, so I decided to set a goal and buy the video game within the next three months with the money I had saved over that time.

When I returned home I developed a budget, listing the items I needed to buy and the amounts needed to pay for them. My parents gave me an allowance each week, and I decided to use some of it to buy school lunch and the rest to save toward the video game purchase. I figured that over the next three months, I would be able to buy my video game and hopefully have money left over.

By the end of the second month, I had over half of the money saved for buying the video game. It was right around the time of Valentine's Day. I wanted to buy gifts for my friends. I needed money, and I needed it fast. So, I thought of the money I had saved for my video game. I figured that because the month wasn't over yet, I could spend some of the savings and still have enough money for the video game by the third month. I spent some of the money on Valentine gifts, and by the time March came around, I had very little money left to pay for the video game. In fact, I didn't even have half the money needed for it because I kept spending the savings on other things when I needed "fast money."

My budgeting was a failure because I didn't stay focused on achieving my goal. Instead of putting my goal of buying my video game as a top priority, I figured that because I had time to save, I would have enough by the end of the third month — this turned out not to be the case.

Looking back, I realize I should have put away some of my allowance for school lunch each week, then split what remained into video game savings and savings for other miscellaneous items. It would then have taken a longer time to save up for the purchase of the video game, but I would not have spent the video game savings.

The lesson I learned from that experience taught me that whenever I set a goal, I should make it my priority and stick with it until I achieve it. Everything went well until I thought the video game wasn't a priority anymore and the Valentines were more important. My budgeting was unsuccessful because I had planned the expenses for the things I needed, but not the funding for the items.

What is a Budget?

A budget is a written plan for your money that takes a look at how much money you have compared to how many expenses you have. It is a relatively simple concept. You first figure out how much money you bring in (your income), and then figure out where your money needs to go. Here is an example:

Maria brings in a monthly income of $290 from her part-time job at the mall. She also gets a monthly allowance of $80 from her parents and usually makes around $40 a month babysitting. As far as expenses go, she is responsible for paying for her lunches at school and putting gas in the car she drives. Her parents pay her car insurance and the car is paid off. Maria does have to pay for the membership fees for the various clubs she belongs to at school, totaling $20 a month, and has to pay for the costumes she wears for dance recitals. The cost of the dance costumes vary, but average out to around $25 a month when spread out over the entire year.

This means that Maria's monthly income is around $410, which is the total of her three income sources combined. Her monthly expenses are a little more complicated. The amount of money she pays for her lunches changes weekly according to what she buys to eat, or if she instead packs her lunch. Her gas expenses vary, too, depending on how much she drives and what the gas prices are at the moment. When she sits down to look at her expenses, she can estimate an average cost for these things and come up with an estimated list of monthly expenses:

- **Lunches:** $80
- **Gas:** $50
- **Memberships:** $20
- **Dance costumes:** $25
- **Total:** $175

So far, Maria has an extra $235 for the month. Knowing that she will want extra spending money, she adds another expense to the budget list:

Entertainment money: $100

Now Maria is down to $135 left over, but don't forget: She still needs to follow the 10 percent rule and put money into her emergency fund.

Emergency fund: $41

This leaves Maria with $94 dollars a month, which she can put away into savings, keep in her checking account, or use to cover other expenses like clothes, school trips, and miscellaneous things that come up. It would be wise for Maria not to leave that $94 floating around and not specify where it should go, though. After all, $94 a month for a full year equals more than $1,100. That is a lot of money to waste, especially considering it equals more than two months' worth of income for Maria.

She has a few choices here. She can add more money to her emergency fund or put money away in another savings account for a specific expense. She can also add more money to her entertainment fund and ease up on her spending restrictions. Another option is to stop babysitting and have more time for herself, which she can afford because of the extra money she has left over when she analyzes her current budget. With whatever option she chooses, she needs to be very intentional in stating where the extra money will go — and not just assume that she'll find somewhere for the money to get spent.

Maria decides to add another line item to her budget: Charitable giving. She intends on giving $20 a month to a charitable cause, such as the local animal shelter or to her church. This leaves $74 a month extra. She wisely decides to split between her emergency fund and her regular savings account, which she is using to save for a road trip she will take with her best friend when they graduate from high school in a couple of years.

Maria is in a good position. Some teens (and adults) find their budget stretched far beyond what their income can handle. Consider this scenario: Steve has a monthly income of $588 from his part-time job at a restaurant. He does not have any other source of income. Although Steve makes more money than Maria, he also has more bills to pay. Here is a list of his monthly bills:

- **Cell phone:** $40
- **Online gaming subscriptions:** $44
- **Cable TV for his bedroom:** $50
- **Car payment and insurance:** $340
- **Gas:** $45
- **Entertainment expenses:** $100
- **Total:** $619

Steve hasn't even put any money into a savings account yet, and already he has budgeted for more than his monthly income. When a written budget looks like this, it is definitely time to make some adjustments. In Steve's case, his biggest expense is his car payment and insurance. He obviously purchased a car that was far out his price range, especially considering he won't even have enough money to make any repairs that are needed if the car breaks down. He can be sure, however, that even if his car isn't working, he will still need to make the payments on time every month or he will find himself in big trouble.

When a budget just doesn't add up, as is the case with Steve, there are two options that can be explored: either bring in more income or reduce spending. A combination of the two options may also work.

How can Steve make this budget work? Although his best bet would be to sell his car, he also has the option of ditching the cable TV in his room and reducing his entertainment expenses. This would still be cutting it close, though, and in reality, most people can't go every long without spending any extra money on miscellaneous items. Everyone wants to be able to go to the movies once in a while or indulge in a concert, so it simply isn't realistic to not have any money at all for these types of expenses.

Steve also has to figure out a way to incorporate saving into his budget. He is setting himself up for financial failure if he keeps budgeting so poorly. If he can't get rid of his car, he needs to drop other expenses and find a way to increase his income. It may be possible to pick up more hours at the restaurant or get a job that pays higher wages. Either way, his current budget isn't working.

Just for the sake of argument, let's say that Steve doesn't sell his car, but instead lowers his expenses substantially and gets a nice raise at work. He is then able to start putting money into a savings account that will come in quite handy if his car needs repairs, and he feels a lot less pressure financially because he's making ends meet and saving for a rainy day.

CASE STUDY: FINANCIAL SACRIFICES

Kelly – High School Student

The world of finances can seem so mysterious. What we forget is that — for the average student — saving money and having financial security is not about large investments and corporate confusion. Rather, the key to successful financial endeavors for teens is being careful with money simply on a day-to-day basis. Managing stocks and business can prove lucrative for some. However, it's been my personal experience that — while trying to juggle my classes, SAT tests, sports, community service, and family obligations — meeting with a stock broker doesn't really fit into my schedule. Instead, I've found that getting scholarships, asking for money instead of gifts, and differentiating your needs from your wants are simple, but extremely effective, ways to not only earn money, but keep it.

I'd like to begin by explaining my experience with financial sacrifices. It is important that anyone trying to be financially prudent understand that being wise with money 1) is a lifestyle and 2) does not come without sacrifices. I say that it is a lifestyle because wisdom — in any form — is not fleeting. If it were, it wouldn't be wisdom. Saving money for a period is helpful, but if one returns to the spending habits that caused them to not have needed money, any efforts to save will have been in vain. I secondly say that it comes with sacrifices because it is difficult to discipline yourself. Especially in the United States, consumerism is hard to fight when everything is marketed so enticingly. With that said, I urge you: Do not ever compromise the things you hold most dear — family, your health, your faith — for the sake of money — ever. When I was in middle school, I thought I would be helping my family save some money by not eating lunch. My mom would write me a check that should have lasted a month, and I made it stretch for two. When she found out what I had done, she was hurt that I had lied to her and worried that I incorrectly believed money came before my wellbeing. My intentions were good from a financial standpoint, but that never justifies hurting those you love.

So, what are some positive ways to earn money? Scholarships are probably the most revered way for teens to earn money, but certainly the most misunderstood. While successful athletes are often offered sports scholarships, I know I can't throw a football well enough to pay my way through college. I won one scholarship in my junior year of high school. I've observed in my four years of high school that scholarships are most often offered to seniors, so keep in mind with your scholarship search that as an underclassman, scholarships are extremely competitive. One way to relieve this pressure is by applying for local scholarships. The scholarship I won was sponsored by a local chapter of the Veterans of Foreign Wars. The scholarship was easy to find because all VFWs around the country do it, but also easy to win because I was only competing against the high school students in my school district. That solitary scholarship was one of many I had applied for that year. Although getting no answer from many scholarship foundations was daunting and saddening, I attribute my win to my strength in numbers. The fact of the matter is, the more times you get your name out there, the more likely you are to win something. One great aspect of local scholarships is they usually pay you in cash or check and pay no mind to what you spend it on. You can use it toward a car payment just as well as you can spend it on a college textbook. As my mom always says about scholarships, even in the worst-case scenario, you work on a scholarship for five hours and you only get $100 — so what? "Honey, I went to college and I don't even get paid $20 an hour!"

Another way I've saved is by asking for money instead of gifts. Wouldn't you rather receive versatile cash than getting a random gift from your great-aunt Betsey? Pick one (small) thing you really want for your birthday, Easter, Christmas, Hanukkah, or any other gift-giving holiday and tell your family that, for you, saving money for (insert expensive item here) is of paramount importance to you. They will appreciate your reasonableness, responsibility, and vocabulary — only aiding your cause. If whatever you are saving money for is something you feel has great significance — a mission trip, college, starting a business — then you shouldn't be afraid to ask friends and family for their support, financially and otherwise. It shows how strongly you feel about your dream that you have the courage to tell people what your goals are. These were my tactics and mindset while raising $3,000 for a summer mission trip to the Philippines. I'm proud to say that in fewer than five months, I'll be in Manila. I owe more or less all of it to choosing financial contributions over material gifts. To me, a ticket to the Philippines to mission is much more valuable than any other gift imaginable.

This brings us to another subject — distinguishing what we want from what we need. I've spent numerous summers at sleep-away camps. I stay for a month or more at a time away from family with girls I don't know, without air-conditioning, without hot water, and I've found that not only do I survive — I truly enjoy the independent, different situations, and I make lots of friends.

How does this relate to finance? Through my experience at camp, I've learned that there are certain things that I can live without — central air conditioning, hot showers, and familiar faces. I've been able to identify the fact that living in a dorm without these things is not only possible to me, but familiar. So, for me, living in a dorm with no central air conditioning is in my best interest because it saves me money each semester.

It is more important to me that I save money for a down payment on a house than spending it on my dorm rent.

Think of the things in your life that you can and can't live without. Make a list so that you can organize your thoughts in a tangible way. Maybe to you, a hot shower is imperative, but you don't feel the need to buy the most popular and up-to-date clothing. Now you know which expenses can be eliminated once your budget tightens.

Saving money is a daily activity whose recompense is hard to quantifiably identify. It is quite easy to get discouraged when the reward is so far off — when you have to force yourself to fill out just one more scholarship application, or stop yourself from buying that beautiful necklace that you know you can live without. More importantly than anything, I've found it essential to always remember what you're saving money for. My personal goal of going to the Philippines, for example, helped me to focus on my aspirations even when there were so many immediately pleasing things that I would have liked to have received for the holidays. I hope that you find what I've learned and experienced to be true and useful when put to practice in your own life.

Create Your Budget

Your budget may not be as complicated as the budgets in the previous section. Maybe your parents cover most of your expenses, so you only have to figure out where to spend your allowance. It is never too early in life to figure out how to budget, and if you can get into the habit of budgeting your money now, you will have a much easier time with money when you become older.

Write it down!

Some people have a loose budget they keep in their minds and never write it down on paper or enter it into a spreadsheet or app. They may tell themselves they can only spend so much on a certain expense and so much on another expense, but they do

not make the effort to put their budget in writing. While it is admirable that they are trying to budget their money, their budgets would most likely be much more effective if they actually took the time to make a *written* budget.

Why is it so important to actually write down your budget? There are a few reasons, but one of the most important reasons is because writing it down allows you to actually look at where your money is going. How are you supposed to tell your money what to do if you don't already know where it is going? By writing down your budget, you not only figure out where your money has already been going, but you can also tell it exactly where you want it to go.

You may be wondering, "What does it mean to figure out where my money has been going? I *know* where I spend my money." Just knowing what store you spend your money at, or having a general understanding of the types of things you spend your money on, does not mean you are in control of your money.

Make no mistake about it; the main goal in personal finance is to *control your money.*

You will find that writing out your budget will help you immensely. Many people have taken the time to write out a budget only to be shocked when they realize how they actually spend their money. When writing down their budget, people who use credit cards often realize they actually spend more money than they make, which is never a good financial situation.

Here is how to write a budget for yourself:

1. **Figure out how much money you make each month.** This can be easy if you make the same amount of money every month. But if your income changes, you should average it out. For example, if you make $500 a month half of the year and $400 a month the other months, your average is $450 dollars a month.

   Write down the total amount you make per month at the top of the paper.

2. **Write down how much money you save each month.** This is the amount of money you put into your savings account and can include both your emergency fund money and any other savings you regularly contribute to. If you don't currently save any money at all, start by writing down 10 percent of your income for this category.

3. **Figure out how much money you owe every month for recurring bills.** Recurring bills are the type of bills you must pay every single month. Examples of these types of bills include cell phone bills, monthly gym membership fees, and car insurance, if this isn't paid by your parents. If you have bills that are only paid once a year, like an annual club membership fee, divide it by 12 and put one month's worth of the expense into this category. If some of your recurring bills vary in price from month to month, average the cost out.

Write down each recurring bill in a list under your total income and savings, then add up the total amount you spend monthly.

4. **Figure out how much money you spend on other expenses**. Estimate how much you spend every month for food, gas for your car, going out with your friends, buying clothes, and anything else you spend money on. This is the category where you would list expenses like your trips to Starbucks or the in app purchases. Don't worry if you don't know the exact amounts. Right now, you are just trying to get a budget started and will probably adjust it plenty of times before you get the numbers right.

Create some categories for these expenses, such as snacks or clothes, and list each of them separately right underneath your recurring bills. Total up these categories, too.

5. **Do the math**. Add up all your expenses, including the recurring bills and the other expenses, then subtract this total number from the income you wrote down in the beginning.

Your budget may look something like this:

Income: $375
Savings:
    Emergency fund: $40
    Other savings: $40
    Total: $80

Recurring bills:

Honor society monthly dues: $5

Netflix membership: $19

Cell phone: $38

Bus pass: $18

Total: $80

Other expenses:

Lunches: $80

Clothes: $40

Books: $20

Movies out: $35

Charitable giving: $20

Music downloads: $20

Total: $215

TOTAL INCOME: $375

TOTAL EXPENSES: $375

The example above is considered a balanced budget, which means the person writing the budget does not spend more money than he or she earns every month and also can account for all the money that comes in and goes out. Another great feature of the above budget is that not only does the person have both an emergency fund and a regular savings account, but he or she also makes room in the budget to buy fun things like books or a night out at the movies. Additionally, there is still room in the budget to give some money to charity, as well.

Don't panic if your first attempt at a written budget does not come out as clean as this example. You may have to move some money around a little to make the numbers come out equally, but keep in mind: Hardly anyone can get a complete budget written correctly in the very first attempt. Think of your first attempt as a rough draft, and be prepared to revise it more than once. It may take a couple of months before you get a budget written that actually works and is balanced, and you will probably constantly revise that budget as new expenses come up or as you make more money. Also, some people suggest first spending a month writing down all the purchases you made during that time period. This will make you more aware of how your money is being spent. From there, compose a budget based on how you would actually like to spend your money. However, you can also complete a rough draft of your budget in the beginning while tracking your spending at the same time.

How do you revise your first draft? If you have the fortunate problem of having more income than expenses, do this:

1. Make sure you are listing all your expenses accurately.

2. Figure out if you can add more money to savings.

3. Add another line item for something you have been wanting to buy, but didn't think you had enough money.

If your first budget draft reveals higher expenses than income, do this:

1. Examine where you might be able to cut back on expenses, such as buying fewer DVDs or spending less on clothing each month.

2. Figure out a way to increase your income.

A budget isn't just a written listing of where your money should be going. It can also be a guideline of how much money you can actually spend. For example, if after writing your budget you realize you don't have enough money to cover all your expenses, write out how much money you can actually afford to spend for the unnecessary expenses, and then stick to that plan.

If you need extra money for a certain expense one month, you must take that money from a different expense. For example, if you have to buy a birthday gift for your friend, but don't have any money budgeted for the gift, you can spend less on coffee to make up the difference.

If you can stay within your budget, you will have mastered a personal financial task that many adults never even manage.

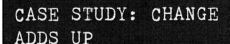

CASE STUDY: CHANGE ADDS UP

Parris – High School Student

In an effort to raise money for college, I've actually gone against all normal money-saving techniques and spent money. How do I save money while spending it? I simply never pay with exact change, and all the change I get back from paying up to the next whole dollar gets put into a jar for college. It may seem like I wouldn't have a lot of money saved from this action, but actually, I've learned quickly that every penny saved adds up quickly.

I'll be keeping at this method until I have all the money saved that I need. This method means every time I go shopping or go out to get lunch, I end up putting a portion of what I spend away toward my college funds.

This is the easiest way I have found to still spend moderately but also be able to put money away toward college every single day. Saving change out of every dollar is also easy to do, and it's a great way to get money from your parents. Change is something many people tend to not care about anymore, so parents usually don't have a problem just giving up whatever comes out of the washer or pennies that they get. Now, though I say I spend and save, I have to be sure I spend wisely. I've made sure to set a limit on how much of my money I spend every week. Instead of going out to dinner with my friends all the time or going to the movies, I've limited myself to only on weekends; that way, I don't just blow money every day.

Another way I save money I will be using toward college is by working and making sure I keep a portion of my paycheck in a savings account. I work up to 30 hours a week, but because I'm still trying to make it through my senior year, my bosses have been great about keeping my schedule during the week down to a minimum and giving me most of my hours during the weekend. Since the New Year, I made it my goal to keep $100 out of every paycheck in an account. Besides keeping all of my change in a jar, I also save $100 out of every check. The hardest part about saving money away is making sure it stays saved. To make sure that I never spend any money that I save, my savings account was made so that I actually can't take money out of it without my mother getting it for me. Though I really hate not being able to access my own money whenever I want, I know that in the long run, it will be so helpful to have all that money put away and kept there, no matter what.

Besides the $100 I put away from every paycheck, if I have any money left over from the last paycheck by the time that the next week comes around, I put that money in my savings account where I won't touch it until it's needed for college. Basically, what I've learned from saving money for college, or anything important, is that if I don't have the cash on me, I won't spend it. Also, I've learned that every penny really does matter. When trying to save money, I just have to keep track of everything I spend and put away all my change, no matter what.

Track Your Spending

Tracking your spending doesn't have to be hard. You don't have to carry a calculator around with you everywhere you go or keep a running tally of every purchase you make. If you can find a tracking method that works well for you — and that you don't mind actually keeping up with —you will soon find that your budget starts to fall right into place.

CASE STUDY: ADVICE FROM A FINANCIAL EXPERT

Andrew Housser — Co-CEO of Bills.com

Here is what you need to know about managing your finances right now:

1. Managing your finances today — no matter how little money you may have — will set the course for your future. Learning to manage finances well will make a difference in an interest rate you get on a car loan or home loan later in life, and may even impact a job search, or whether you get a particular apartment.

2. Managing your finances means you're more likely to have financial freedom sooner in life. It also means you will have choices to do what you want.

3. It's about goals. It's hard to get somewhere if you don't know where you're going. Write down your short-term and long-term goals, which might range from having time to practice for a sport or buying an iPod to saving for college. Once you have goals in mind, you can budget for those goals and adjust accordingly. Saving with a specific goal in mind is much more achievable.

4. Budgeting. Learn what a budget is and how to create and use one.

5. The importance of saving. Making a habit of saving a percentage of every single check, no matter if it comes from a birthday gift or a part-time job, will make a huge difference in life. Aim for 10 percent, but any percent saved, consistently, will make a difference.

6. Pay bills on time; in full, every bill, all the time. Live within your means.

Cash envelopes

One of the easiest and best options for tracking your spending and making sure you stay within your budget is a cash envelope system. This system only works if you use cash instead of a debit card or credit card, but it is really easy and highly effective. This works well for people who already use cash for all their purchases or for people who feel like they spend too much when they use a card.

$ave $mart Tip

When using an envelope system, use sturdy envelopes instead of thin paper envelopes so you aren't constantly replacing them.

Here is how a cash envelope system works:

1. Gather enough envelopes to match every budget item you have. For example, you will have one envelope for lunch money, one envelope for clothes money, and so on. Label each envelope with the budget item it represents. If an envelope is for gas money, write "Gas Money" on the outside of the envelope.

2. Withdraw cash from your account for the amount of money you have budgeted for each item. For example, if you budgeted $15 a week to buy snacks at school, put $15 into the "Snack" envelope. You can also choose to put $60 in the "Snack" envelope if you've budgeted on a monthly basis instead of weekly. Keep in mind: You may be less tempted to spend all your money up front if you only withdraw what you need for a week.

3. When you make a purchase, take the money directly out of whatever envelope corresponds with the purchase. For example, if you buy gas for your car, the money should be taken out of the "Gas" envelope to make the purchase. If you buy a snack at school, the money should come out of the "Snack" envelope. If there is any change left over after you make your purchase, it should go right back into the envelope it came out of. So, if you pull a $5 bill out of the "Snack" envelope to buy a $1 cookie, $4 should go back into the same envelope. Don't put the money back into your wallet. This system only works if you keep the money where it belongs according to your budget. Don't carry all your envelopes with you all the time; only take the money you need with you.

4. If you run out of money from a particular envelope, you know you have met your spending budget for that particular expense. If you want to stick to your budget, you shouldn't pull money from another envelope to restock the depleted one. In the beginning stages of using the envelope system, you may find yourself adjusting how much money goes into each envelope, so don't be surprised if you have

to shift cash around a little. Make note of any changes you make so you can adjust your budget accordingly.

5. At the end of the month, take a look at how much money you have left in your envelopes. You should also take note of how quickly you ran out of money from specific envelopes. By keeping track of these things, you should have no problem figuring out if your budget works and if the amount of money you allow yourself to spend for specific expenses is realistic.

The pros and cons of the cash envelope system

There are both pros and cons to using a cash envelope system. The most important thing is whether or not this system works *for you*. It is unlikely you will continue using a system you don't like or you don't think works very well. The following are a few pros and cons about the system.

Pro: It is really easy to monitor how your money is being spent because you can actually watch the cash disappear from the envelopes. This method is very different than using a credit card or debit card. With a card, your money is abstract because you can't see or touch it.

Con: Sometimes using cash instead of a credit card or debit card can slow things down. People at cash registers have grown accustomed to people swiping a card to make purchases, so using cash may take just a little longer as the clerk counts back your change. The extra time is so little, however, that this really should not be a deciding factor against using a cash envelope system.

Pro: You will probably wind up spending less if you pay with cash from an envelope. When you use a debit card to make purchases, you never actually see the money. You are more likely to think purchases through when you actually have to part ways with the cash. It causes you to ponder, "Do I really need to make this purchase, or would I rather save my money for something better?" Suppose you have $5 left in your "snack" envelope, but three days until the envelope will be refilled. In this situation, you will probably be much less likely to splurge on a $4 smoothie because you know that this purchase will almost wipe out the money you have left. To the contrary, with a credit card or debit card, you may not even realize you only have $5 left until after you have already bought the smoothie.

Con: If you misplace the cash, it's gone. Suppose you lose your envelope containing a week's worth of lunch money. Unless you are really lucky and someone finds the envelope and returns it to you, there is a good chance you will never see that money again. You have to be extra careful about keeping track of your envelopes because losing an envelope usually means losing the money too. You also have to find a secure place to put the envelopes. For example, if you have a brother who likes to go through your wallet and take money without permission, you will need to find a spot to stash the envelopes without his knowing where they are. You also don't want to carry envelopes around that you don't really need. Don't carry all your envelopes in your backpack to school if you only need access to the "lunch money" envelope.

Pro: It's easy to adjust your spending when you use cash envelopes. If you don't have enough money in your "gas" envelope to get you through the end of the week, but you do have extra money in your "movie night" envelope, take the money you need for gas from the movie night envelope. Unfortunately, this will mean you will have to skip the night out at the movies. Keep track of any money transfers so you know what adjustments to make to your budget the next time payday rolls along.

Con: Having envelopes full of money may give you the illusion that you actually have more to spend than you do. Keep a close eye on how much money is actually in your envelopes when using this system.

It isn't necessary to physically carry the envelopes with you when you plan to make a purchase. If you know you'll need $6 for lunch, take that amount out of the envelope and put it in your wallet or pocket. It should be used for lunch and nothing else. Any change from the lunch money should go back into the appropriate envelope. Remember: The cash envelope system doesn't work if you don't keep track of which envelope the cash goes into. Otherwise, they are just a bunch of envelopes stuffed with cash that you can use with reckless abandon. That's not smart money management at all.

Cash envelope systems work well when they are used to both track spending and to stay within your budget. It is a good idea to take a look at how much money you have left in your envelopes (if any) when the times comes to put more money in because this will give you a good idea of where your money is going.

CASE STUDY: LEARNING ABOUT BUDGETING

Christina — High School Student

I have recently learned to set a budget. Four weeks ago, I started my first job, and I have received three paychecks. Out of those paychecks, I have to save 60 percent. Right now, I don't have debt, but soon I will have a car, and with a car comes insurance and gas that I will have to pay for. I also have college to think about. I have to build my savings for college because I want to go to a major university.

My plan is to first save the 60 percent my parents tell me I have to, and then I have to learn to make good choices in the things I spend the rest of my money on. Second, if I can, I will save more of the 40 percent I have left. Right now, my parents make sure I have food and clothes, so there isn't much else that I need. So honestly, I can save more. Third, I have 2 ½ years until I graduate high school; I want to have $6,000 saved from my jobs. Then, if I get scholarships, I should be all right for a few years. Last, in order for me to be where I want to be in the future, I need to stick to the plan now.

In the end, making a budget and saving is not easy, but it is necessary if you want to achieve your goals!

Spending logs

Spending logs are lists that show how much you spend and what you spend your money on. With spending logs, it doesn't matter how you pay for things, as long as you keep track of what you are spending. Spending logs can require a lot more work than using a cash envelope system, but with this system, you get to choose how you pay for things, and you aren't limited to paying for things in cash all the time. For this reason, spending logs are great for people who do not want to be limited to using cash for all their purchases. You can use a debit card, or even a credit card, to buy things, but you have to write down every bit of money you spend. You can decide whether to have separate spending logs for cash or credit, but for many people, the simplified version of one spending log works best.

You have the option of creating your own spending log or buying one that is already formatted from an office supply store. You can also use an Excel spreadsheet or an app like Mint or You Need a Budget to track your spending. This software will even create graphs to show you how you spend your money. If you are a visual learner, a program like this might be helpful to you because it will present all the information to you in a visual form that is easy to understand.

If you don't want to use money management software, then you need another way to record your spending. Some people carry a notebook and record all the purchases they make as they make them, while others keep their purchase receipts throughout the day and then write everything down when they get home. For example, if you spend $1.87 on a soda and a candy bar, you would record "$1.87: soda and candy" in the notebook. Some preprinted spending logs are designed with columns that allow you to write down the category your purchase falls into, which may make it easier for you when trying to determine what adjustments you need to make to your written budget.

Spending logs are of little use if you don't actually take the time to analyze your spending. At the end of the month or week (whichever length of time you decide to use; it's up to you), look at the spending log and determine in which categories you are spending your money. Ask yourself, "Am I spending my money wisely, or am I wasting most of it on stuff I don't need?"

Follow these steps to analyze your spending log:

1. Write down the categories from your budget on a piece of paper.

2. Categorize the spending listed on your log according to the categories from your budget.

3. Add up the money you spent in each category and write down this amount.

4. Look at the total amount you spent compared to the amount you budgeted. How close are the amounts? If you went over budget, the amount will be more than the amount on your written budget. If you went under budget, the amount will be less than the amount on your written budget. Keep in mind: The amounts rarely come out exactly even, but if they do, you should commend yourself for not only writing a realistic budget, but for sticking to your budget so well.

You should also look at what specific purchases you made. Your spending log may reveal that you spent a lot of money on a particular expense, especially if it is a recurring expense, like lunch or daily snacks. You may not have realized you were spending so much on that one category. This may help you make wiser purchasing decisions if you are running out of money quickly or spending money on items you don't really need. You may also be surprised to find that some of your expenses aren't as costly as you once thought. For example, you may think you spend a ton of money on gas, but once you begin using your spending log, you might realize you don't spend nearly as much as you think. This is good news. It will open up more money in your budget for other expenses.

It's important to remember there is nothing wrong with buying things you want as long as you can afford it. In other words, don't beat yourself up over buying an extra-large popcorn instead of the small popcorn at the movie theater if you can indeed afford to pay for the larger popcorn and you won't waste it. Things like sharing a big tub of popcorn with your friends is the kind of expense you should be able to make room for in your budget — as long as you aren't ignoring other necessary expenses to make room for the popcorn.

$ave $mart Tip

"Any time you get money from any source, put 10 percent of that in your savings account immediately. Over time, you will never miss it, and it is a lot of fun to watch it grow."

Christopher Lawson, private wealth advisor

Don't mistake this advice as permission to run around buying whatever your heart desires, though. It is important to remember that while you should be able to enjoy the money you earn, you need to learn how to manage it effectively. *First* learn to manage your money, then learn to enjoy it.

Sample spending log

Date	Amount Spent	Purpose
11/12	$4.00	Smoothie @ The Smoothie Shop
11/12	$14.33	Gas for the car @ A-OK Gas Station
11/13	$5.00	December Membership Dues: Honor Society
11/15	$6.41	Breakfast @ The Egg Cafe

Try keeping a spending log for the first month after you write your budget. Keeping an accurate spending log will reveal to you if you actually spend money like you think you do. Chances are, you don't realize where all your money goes or how much you actually spend. If, after this first month, you decide that a spending log isn't for you, you can explore some of the other options for tracking your spending, but you will probably still learn quite a bit about your spending habits just by keeping the log for a month.

Cards

Some people just don't like to use cash for purchases. If the thought of using a cash envelope system made you cringe and the idea of keeping a written spending log made you want to close this book and walk away, a card system for tracking spending may be best for you.

Did You Know?

Prepaid debit and credit cards have notoriously high fees. While not all prepaid cards feature fees, some gobble up balances quickly. If you buy a prepaid card, make sure to read the information accompanying the card so you know you aren't buying something that will wind up costing you a lot of money.

To use this system, you will need to have a debit or a credit card. It doesn't matter if the card is a traditional credit card, store credit card, prepaid credit card, or a debit card, as long as you receive a statement for your spending on a regular basis. This method is best for people who have access to cards for spending and who are willing to carefully monitor their own spending. Before the card system is explained, read through the explanations for the different types of cards that can be used:

Debit cards are issued by your bank or credit union. They may have a Visa or MasterCard logo on them, but they aren't actually credit cards, which are explained below. Instead, they are attached to your checking account. These are different from ATM cards that are sometimes issued to account holders who do not qualify for a debit card through the regulations of the financial institution. Each time you use the debit card to make a purchase, the amount of money needed for the purchase is directly debited from your account. For example, if you swipe your debit card at the store to buy a $19 DVD, that $19 is taken immediately from your account by the merchant, and that amount of money is no longer available to you. If, before you purchased the DVD, your bank account balance was $200, once you purchased the $19 DVD with your debit card, your account balance immediately became $181.

Prepaid debit cards aren't attached to your checking account, but instead are attached to a balance initially loaded on the card when the card was purchased — whether your parents bought you the card as a gift or you bought it for yourself. These cards are similar to gift cards that can be purchased through specific stores. The main difference is that these cards contain a Visa or MasterCard logo, which means they can be used at multiple stores, rather than just the one store the card was purchased at. These cards are similar to a traditional debit card in the sense that you can only spend the amount of money that is available to you; however, these cards are not attached to an account at a financial institution. For example, suppose your parents buy you a prepaid debit card from a store or financial institution in the amount of $50. As long as there are no fees associated with the card charged against the balance, you'll have $50 available to spend. You swipe the card at a store and the amount of the purchase is deducted from your available balance. If you buy the $19 DVD with your $50 prepaid debit card, your card will then have $31 available.

Some prepaid cards are reloadable, which means you can add more money to the balance anytime. Not all cards are like this. On non-reloadable cards, once you have spent the full balance, the card is no longer usable. Prepaid debit cards are also sometimes referred to as prepaid credit cards, which are the same concept and are not real credit cards.

Credit cards and store credit cards (credit cards that can only be used at the store that issued you the card) are revolving accounts, which means you borrow money from an available balance given to you by a credit card company every time you make a purchase. When you buy something using the card, that amount of money is subtracted from the total amount you have available to you. When you make a payment, your available spending balance goes up. Most credit cards come with a set available spending limit. After you apply for the credit card and are approved, the credit card company sends you a card and specifies that you can only spend up to a certain amount. Suppose you obtain a credit card with a $500 credit limit. This means you are able walk into a store and spend a total of $500, but you cannot spend more than that. If you try to spend more than your credit limit, two things could happen. First, the purchase may be rejected or declined. Or, the purchase will be accepted, but you will be charged massive fees for spending beyond the limit set by the company.

Credit cards, debit cards, or prepaid debit cards are a great way to track your spending because a record of purchases made is kept by the bank or credit card company. Each month, you will receive a statement in the mail, online, or through e-mail allowing you to review exactly how you spent your money. You will be able to see where and when you made a purchase and how much money you spent. However, the statement will not show you the specific items you bought at a store. It's important to keep track of the individual items you purchased if using a credit card statement to track your spending.

In most cases, you won't have to wait for a statement by mail in order to view your purchases. Most cards, whether traditional or prepaid, will allow you to access your account online any time of the day. This is really handy for monitoring your spending because, for most people, it is a lot easier to remember why you spent money at a certain store if you look within a few days of making the purchase instead of a few weeks afterwards. To find out if your card has this feature, visit the website for the company that issued the card or talk to a customer service representative. The customer service telephone number can often be found on the back of the card. You will also likely receive information about setting up an online account when you receive your card in the mail. Once you find the correct website, you will need to set up an online account before you can look at your spending log.

Some financial institutions offer programs that track your spending for you or allow you to export your spending information to another program on your computer that tracks your spending. For example, most financial institutions will have an option on their website to export your spending information to your money management software, such as Excel. Linked accounts on Mint automatically track all of this information. Using this feature can save you a lot of time and effort.

You'll analyze this information just like you would if you had maintained a written spending log, although if you use money management software to keep track of your spending, there will be a lot less work involved. If you use your card to obtain cash from an ATM or ask for cash back when making a purchase at a cash register, you will need to manually record the purchase in your check register or spending log and notate what you used the money for when you are reviewing all your card purchases. In fact, if you withdraw a lot of cash out using your card, you may find yourself in a situation where you need to keep a separate spending log for your cash withdrawals. By keeping a separate log of purchases made with cash, you will have an easier time analyzing your purchases at the end of the month. Even if you have a budget category for "spending money" and plan to withdraw cash for this category, you need to know what you're spending it on and why.

When you analyze your purchases at the end of the month, ask yourself whether you are spending too much and not saving enough. Ask yourself if you spend too impulsively, or if you are as careful as you should be with your money.

There is one important thing you need to know about using cards to make purchases, regardless of whether you're using a debit card attached to a bank account or another type of card: You will probably spend more using a card than you will if you use cash. It's too easy to just hand over a card to make a purchase without really looking at the total amount you spent. Even adults have a hard time with the concept of using plastic as money. They know the money will be debited from their account or the amount of the purchase will be added to the total amount of money they owe to their credit card company, but psychologically, it just isn't the same thing as paying with cold hard cash.

$ave $mart Tip

"Start saving right now. Even if it is a dollar a week or month, you should begin making this a habit. As you get older, you will have more to save and you will be in the habit. Snowballs start small, but if you keep rolling them they get bigger and bigger. It is responsible to live within your means. Overspending is like overeating, it leads to many problems that have no easy solutions."

Ken Washer, DBA, CFA, CFP, associate professor of finance
Creighton University

Never underestimate the psychological factor associated with spending money. If you notice you spend more money with cards than you do with cash — even if you tell yourself you won't spend more than you plan on spending — it may be time to stop using cards and switch to paying only with cash. That's the great thing about managing your own finances: You're in charge, and if you know something isn't working well, you can switch it up to something that works better.

Checkbook Registers

No matter how you decide to keep track of your spending, you should always stay up-to-date on your checkbook register if you maintain a checking account. Maintaining a checkbook register allows you to always know how much money you have available in your checking account. Your financial institution will give you a checkbook register when you open your account, and in this register, you should record any transaction, whether it's a deposit, a withdrawal, or a fee. Here is an example of a checkbook register:

Check #	Date	Description	With-drawal	Deposit	Balance
	11/23	ATM Withdrawal	$20.00		$453.22
112	11/23	Galore Bookstore	$12.68		$440.54
	11/26	A-OK Gas Station	$22.97		$417.57
	11/26	Paycheck		$400.00	$817.57
113	11/28	Car Payment	$194.25		$623.32
	11/28	Phones & More	$14.99		$608.33

Your checkbook register is used to keep track of debits and credits to your checking account. It is different from a spending log in the sense that it only keeps track of your checking account activity and does not record anything you buy with cash. Even though a checkbook register is not a complete spending log, it is still important to keep it accurate and up-to-date. If you don't know how much money is in your account, you may make a mistake and wind up writing a check that you don't have money in the account to cover.

Deciding how to track your spending

Which method should you use to track your spending? It's a good idea to start with whatever method seemed most appealing to you when you were reading through the descriptions. If you give it a try and don't like it, you can try a different one. Your parents may also have great tips regarding how you should track your spending, especially if they actively track their spending on a regular basis. Depending on your spending habits, you may wind up creating a totally different tracking method comprised of a mixture of all three methods, or you may even create a method that is completely unique. It doesn't really matter which method you use, as long as you are actually tracking your spending and learning how to effectively manage your spending. Tracking your spending tells you where your money is going and reveals to you important things that you may need to change. For example, you may not realize you waste a lot of your money until you actually make the effort to track how it's being spent. You might also discover you can afford to save more money, or you have enough money left over each month to contribute generously to a charitable cause that you care about. You'll never know these things unless you take the time to take a good look at how you spend.

If you still aren't sure about which tracking method you should try, answer these questions:

- Are you willing to use cash for all your purchases? If so, start with the cash envelope system.

- Are you good at keeping written records? If so, start with the spending log system.

- Are you looking for the most convenient way to track your spending? Can you avoid making impulse purchases? If so, start with the card system, utilizing money management software to assist you.

There is nothing wrong with deciding that one method doesn't work for you and trying another method instead. A lot of managing personal finance is trial and error, so if one method doesn't work for you, don't stress. It isn't an indication that you can't handle your money. You can handle your money; you just need to find the way that works best for you.

CASE STUDY: TAKING CONTROL OF YOUR FINANCES
Amy — High School Student

It is an exciting, and also somewhat frightening, time when you begin taking control of your own finances. Taking responsibility of your money and what you must spend it on is key. When one reaches the point where they are able to put aside personal desires and concentrate on their necessities, it is a defining moment.

I currently work as a cashier at a grocery store and babysit a few nights a week. The process of filling out job applications and attending interviews was very extensive. Over the course of one month, I filled out over a dozen applications. I went to clothing stores, restaurants, grocery stores, and other various businesses and attended four interviews.

While much of my time was spent unsuccessfully searching for a place of employment, this experience proved beneficial. I found out, as each interview progressed, that dressing professionally and carrying myself in a modest manner made others show respect toward me.

With the money that I make from cashiering and babysitting, I pay for my gas, car payment, and insurance payment. I know the total I will spend each month, and I am responsible for making sure I have that amount in my checking account. Each time I receive a paycheck, I put aside a small amount for unexpected expenses and am aware of what I have left over for personal satisfaction. There have been instances that occurred where I had to use money from savings, such as having a flat tire, and I was grateful for having money put aside.

A major part of balancing finances is to know when it is acceptable to spend money and when it is not. Let's say you were to buy breakfast every morning before school and spent five dollars for a coffee and a breakfast sandwich. $5 may not seem like a lot of money, but when you multiply it by five days a week, then four weeks a month, you have spent $100 on breakfast when you could have eaten a bowl of cereal and drunk a cup of coffee before leaving your house in the morning. It is nice to buy things for yourself occasionally, but it is extremely important to know when it is appropriate.

Having a job and paying bills during high school has proved to be a great learning experience. From having a checking account and debit card, I have learned the true meaning of responsibility, as well as self-control. I feel like I am now a mature young adult who is able to determine what is truly important.

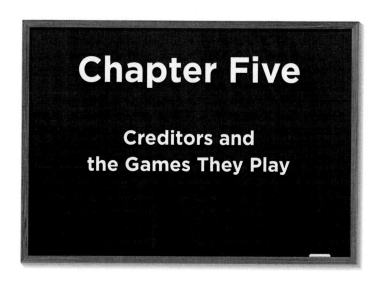

Chapter Five

Creditors and the Games They Play

C redit is the term used to describe the act of lending money to someone, and it is big business. Don't ever think a company is offering you a credit card because they truly want to help you learn about managing credit, or because they want to do you some sort of favor. This is how many credit card companies market themselves to young people. Offering credit is a money-making venture, and it has nothing to do with trying to help people. It is all about making a profit.

This doesn't mean that creditors are evil or mean; it just means that creditors make their money by getting you to spend yours. In the vast majority of instances, creditors aren't doing anything illegal. They are merely offering a product to consumers and earning money when the consumers utilize the product. If you have heard your parents or other people say that banks are evil or credit card companies aren't fair, these adults may just be frustrated about credit as a whole. Credit card companies aren't evil — they're just out to make as much money as possible.

The Principles of Credit

So what is credit? Credit involves lending money to someone and expecting the money to get paid back eventually. For example, if your mother lets you borrow $20 but specifies that she wants it paid back within a week, she is extending credit to you by offering you a loan. In other words, she assumes that the $20 is a safe loan because she assumes you will pay it back. If you don't pay it back by the deadline, she may give you some sort of penalty — like not lending you money the next time you ask, or giving you extra chores to make up for the money. This is similar to what creditors do. They lend you money that they believe you will pay back in a timely manner, and if you don't pay back the money when you should, you wind up paying extra.

There is usually a cost involved with using credit, whether it's through fees or interest. Don't confuse interest you pay to a credit card company with the interest you earn from a savings account. It is very different. You already know that interest earned on a savings account can be compared to a "thank you" from the financial institution for allowing them access to your money. Interest charged on credit accounts, on the other hand, is more like a "thank you" that you pay the creditor for giving you access to the money on your credit card. Remember: Credit is a type of loan given to you by the creditor. Creditors charge interest as a way of making a profit on the money they are lending you. The interest you are charged on your credit account can pile up quickly because compound interest applies with credit interest just as it does with interest you earn from a savings account. Do you remember compound interest from the section about savings accounts in Chapter 3? If not, review this section again.

While compound interest is great when involved with savings accounts, it isn't so great when dealing with credit accounts. The interest builds up quickly, and with a credit account, you have to pay that interest back. In other words, the longer you take to pay off your credit card balance, the more interest your account will accumulate, and the more money you will wind up paying in the long run.

Fees come in many different forms, but can be summed up as extra expenses added to the balance you owe but are not a direct result of a purchase you make. For example, suppose you use a credit card to buy a jacket at a clothing store. The credit limit on your card is $200, but the jacket costs $225. You decide to buy the jacket, even though it costs $25 more than you have available on your card. The purchase goes through, but your credit card company adds a fee to your balance as a penalty for spending more than your credit limit. In this example, if the over-the-limit fee is $20, your credit card balance will then be $245, which is the cost of the jacket ($225) plus the fee added by the credit card company ($20).

Fees don't just come in the form of penalties. Some credit cards companies charge fees for routine maintenance to your account, such as submitting an application for the card in the first place. Other fees that you may run into are monthly usage fees, annual fees, and fees for speaking to customer service representatives at the credit card company for issues that you might be able to solve using an automated system (either over the phone or using the computer). The good news is that credit card companies are required to explain every fee to you in a terms and conditions brochure. This document is usually mailed when you receive your new card and available online, and it explains every instance that may potentially result in an extra fee. For this reason, you cannot claim that you didn't know something would result in a fee. The bad news is that some creditors charge fees for far too many things. Do you want a copy of your statement? Get ready to pay a fee. Do you need another card because yours went through the washing machine? You'll pay a fee. Always keep in mind that credit card companies, along with all the other types of creditors, are involved in money-making ventures. Remember: Creditors earn money when they charge you interest and fees. If they can legally charge you a fee for something, they will probably try. Luckily, credit card laws are evolving, and it is becoming more difficult for lenders to charge really high fees. This won't, however, stop these companies from charging *all* fees.

Common credit card fees include:

- **Application fees**: These are fees some credit card companies charge people for submitting an application for a credit card.

- **Maintenance fees**: These include annual or monthly fees charged for nothing more than having the account open and active. Not all credit cards have these fees, and you should avoid cards with them if possible.

- **Penalty fees**: These fees are charged when you do something with the account that you aren't supposed to, such as making your payment late or exceeding your preset credit limit. These fees can add up quickly, so always make your payments on time, and don't exceed your spending limit.

- **Transaction fees**: This includes fees for obtaining cash from your credit card instead of using the card for purchases or transferring one credit card balance to another card, which is called a balance transfer.

Because credit card fees can really add up, your parents may get upset with you if you misuse a credit card they have given you. They don't want to pay a bunch of extra fees imposed by the credit card company on top of the balance you charge up. If you misuse a credit card given to you by a parent, your parents will wind up not only paying for whatever purchases you made, but also for any extra fees incurred because of the way you used the card. Of course, if they hold you responsible for your own spending, they won't be the ones paying for all these extra fees — you will.

If you're under 18, the time when you start acquiring your own credit cards and loans in your own name is right around the corner. It won't be long before you are solely responsible for any credit you obtain without needing your parents' permission. The more you learn about how credit works and how to manage your credit without losing all your money, the better.

If you are already of legal age to obtain credit, you have undoubtedly been approached by creditors looking to get you to apply — especially if you are a college student. Creditors love to offer credit to students for a few different reasons:

1. You may still get money from your parents, so if you get behind in your payments, they'll probably help you out.

2. Because this may be your first time handling credit on your own, you are more likely to charge up the credit card quickly and pay a great deal in interest rate charges and fees. You will probably also accept a higher initial interest rate due to a lack of credit history.

3. If you complete your degree program and find a high-paying job, the credit card company is hoping you will remain a lifelong account holder.

This isn't what the credit card companies will tell you, though. Instead, they will use tactics to lure you into applying for credit that you may not even need.

The Tactics

You already know that credit is big business, but you should also know that you are big business to creditors. It's true; if they can lure you in at an early age, not only will they grab you when you may not have learned enough about managing credit to avoid extra fees and high interest rates, but they also hope to keep you as a customer for years to come.

Instead of falling prey to the marketing tactics used by creditors, learn how to spot the tactics beforehand so you aren't tricked into getting credit you don't really need.

Look out!

Creditors spend a lot of money on marketing and research to find out how to entice teenagers and college students into applying for a credit card, and the tactics they come up with extend far beyond the commercials you see on TV or the ads you see in online. By now, you probably realize you're being advertised a product when you see commercials for credit cards. There may be times, however, when their marketing techniques are not so obvious. Remember, marketers spend hours researching nothing but ways to get you to spend your money — and their tactics may not be so easy to resist. If you are heading off to college, brace yourself; creditors will approach you left and right. Opportunities to apply for credit won't only come in the mail; they'll approach you while just walking down the street. If you aren't old enough to apply for credit on your own yet, the same marketing tactics that will be used on you when you are an adult are probably already being used on you now. Credit card companies want to influence your thoughts and behavior now so you will want to apply for credit once you are able to. Look out for the following tactics because, oftentimes, these tactics are used by creditors not offering the best interest rates and terms with their credit. They often must resort to other tactics to entice applicants. These companies know that under normal circumstances, you wouldn't want to apply for their card due to high interest rates and fees, so they have to figure out other ways to get your attention.

Here, have something for free

One day, you notice a table with a bunch of people around it, busily filling out some paperwork and talking with a really excited representative. Everyone walking away from the table leaves with a really cool shirt, hat, or some other item that probably features the local college's mascot or some other design, making it look like the school is endorsing the promotion.

What form is everyone filling out so eagerly? The representative is someone who works for a credit card company, and the form is an application for a credit card. Fill out an application for a credit card, get a free shirt. It seems easy enough, and some students don't even think they will wind up getting approved for the credit card to begin with, so getting a free shirt seems harmless enough. That free shirt, however, can cost you plenty if you get approved for the card and start using it. All the interest and fees you will wind up with will cost much more than the credit card company spent on the shirt. How much more? Think of it this way: The shirt probably cost the company less than a dollar to produce, but the credit card can potentially cost you hundreds (or even thousands) of dollars in the long run.

This tactic was once common on college campuses, but today, some colleges and universities do not allow credit card companies to advertise on campus. There were just too many instances of college students getting into serious trouble with debt, which affected their success as college students and, in turn, lowered the success and graduation rates of the institution. College leadership does not generally like companies coming to their campuses and wreaking havoc among the students, but for some colleges, it was a tough decision to make because credit card companies paid colleges a lot of money to be able to come on campus and offer credit cards to students. For this reason, don't be surprised if you do run into something like this when you head off to college. While some college leaders don't really like the idea of students falling deep into debt, they also don't like the idea of losing money the credit card companies give them.

It isn't only on college campuses where you might run into a table filled with credit card applications and free stuff. You might find the same tactic used at stores in the mall: Fill out an application, get a free backpack! Some charities will use this same tactic as well. For example, you might take a trip to the zoo and find a table outside the admission gate: Get a card, and a portion of your purchases will be donated to the animal foundation. The same often happens at restaurants where young adults frequently visit: Apply for a card, and get a free pizza. They want you to feel like you're getting something for free, or you're somehow helping out by applying for a credit card. Signs that say, "Show your school spirit with a mascot credit card!" shouldn't make you want to apply for a credit card. Instead, they should make you laugh because you know racking up debt has nothing to do with school spirit.

This tactic doesn't only come in the form of a table with a smiling representative. You might get applications in the mail promising you free stuff, or you might see site banners online meant to pique your interest. You shouldn't apply for a credit card based on one promise or one advertisement. Instead, you should search among several different credit cards, and if the best one just so happens to offer a cool shirt or an automatic donation to your favorite school or charity, it's a nice bonus. Keep in mind, though, that the best credit cards don't really have to offer you anything like that in order to be the best option for you.

Here, let us help you

It can be tough when you are first trying to build credit. Some creditors just don't want to take a chance on you because you don't have any credit history at all. Not having credit history means you have not yet opened up any credit accounts in your name. Due to your lack of credit history, they don't know whether you're going to make payments on time, or if you're going to be the type of customer they have to chase to get their money back. In fact, if you aren't a college student and you don't have any previous credit, you may have a really hard time getting approved for a decent deal on a credit card.

Credit card companies know young people often get turned down when they first start applying for credit, and they also know many young people are frustrated by this. For this reason, their marketing tactic is to try to appear as though they are out to help young people establish credit. They make promises such as "Let us help you establish credit!" or "We guarantee approval, even without a credit history!" They try to make it seem like they are looking out for your best interests, and helping you build credit is their main priority. While it may be true that their target consumers are young people who do not yet have credit, this *does not* mean they're doing it out of the goodness of their hearts. They're doing it because they have decided they can make the most money on young people who have little experience with responsibly managing their money. Credit card companies and other lenders are never your buddies. While it's true that there are usually some very nice people who work for these companies, when their workday ends they really couldn't care less whether you are overspending or getting in over your head. It's their job to entice you to spend your money — and they get a bonus if you spend it with their company. It is highly unlikely the people who make the major decisions at these companies are really on some sort of mission to genuinely help people who need to establish credit. They're out to make money, and that's it.

You won't just run into this situation with credit cards. Lenders for car loans commonly use this tactic, too, so don't be surprised if you see signs at car dealerships that say things like "No Credit, No Problem!" or "Let Us Help You Get Financed!" Again, these lenders are out to make money. They're not out to hold your hand and guide you toward financial independence. Don't fall for it.

Here, buy anything you want

Most people like to have nice things, and you probably aren't an exception to this rule. There is nothing wrong with wanting to have stylish clothes, the latest electronics, and a nice car, but there is something wrong with getting it all before you can afford it.

Credit card companies that market to young people know a large portion of young adults do not really understand the fundamentals of using credit, such as the fact that interest is charged on balances that aren't paid off in full every time the credit card bill arrives. Instead of appealing to young people with promises of low interest rates or low fees, credit card companies try to appeal to young people's desire to get all the nice things they want right now.

You will run into this a lot when you are shopping at a mall. Your favorite retailers will have signs up all over the store urging you to open up a credit card account and get access to money in the account instantly. This means you can apply for a credit card, get approved, and walk out of the store with a bag full of merchandise — without paying a dime out of your pocket. They may even offer you a 10 percent discount on the purchases you make that day only, enticing you to spend as much as you can right up front. What some people don't realize, however, is that the bill for the purchase will show up soon and, if the balance is not paid in full before the due date, interest is going to start piling up.

Even if the store offers you a discount on your purchase, the discount you get won't make much of a difference if you don't pay the balance in full. If you only make the minimum payment required each month, you'll get charged interest and fees that will probably cost much more than the discount you received for opening the account to begin with. Don't assume because the card can only be used at one particular store that store credit cards are not as dangerous as Visa or MasterCard credit cards. You can still rack up significant debt using these cards, and if you don't make your payments on time, they can still hurt your credit score.

If you get a little confused when reading about interest rates, discounts, fees, and how they all interact with each other, don't worry; it can all be summed up in this simple statement: Don't buy things you can't afford. Don't feel like you're weird if you have strong feelings about wanting nice things — most people have these same desires. Even adults have these feelings. When it comes to your personal finances, though, you need to realize that instant credit can be an instant problem. Yes, you can get your hands on the things you want to have without having to shell out any money initially, but what happens when your bills start coming in? In fact, there are some people who will buy something with a credit card, use that item up, and discard it — and then still wind up paying on that same purchase long after they don't even have the item anymore. Do you really want to take months (or perhaps years) to pay for a shirt you wore once and then gave away? Doesn't it seem a little ridiculous to have to keep making payments for something that you don't even own anymore? This is what happens when you use credit to buy the things you want, instead of buying with cash or a debit card.

$ave $mart Tip

> Don't use the characters you see on TV or in the movies as a realistic view of the things you should have. Just because a character on your favorite show wears designer clothes or has expensive electronics does not mean that this is realistic for you. Falling into this trap will get you deep into debt quickly.

Think back to the section you've already read about needs versus wants. When you indulge in your wants and use credit to get them, you're setting yourself up for financial problems.

CASE STUDY: YOUR FIRST CREDIT CARD

Tori — High School Student

"This is for emergencies only." That's what my parents told me when they handed me my very own credit card that drew money straight from their account. I was so excited! No longer did I have to wait for my parents to fish out cash to give me when I went out. I had it right at my command! Trips to the mall, the movies, out to eat — it was all going to be so carefree now! Turns out, I was right. It was carefree...for me. But when my parents saw the bill, it ended up that my definition of an emergency"was a bit different than theirs.

That's when my parents decided it was time for me to start managing my own finances. Of course, after the previous credit card spending, I was in for a big shock. My parents promptly took me to the bank and helped me set up a student checking account. Although I was disappointed that I no longer had a huge pool of money at my disposal, the independence of my new account was exciting. I got my own checks and my own debit card, complete with my very own picture. I was now responsible for paying my own bills — eating out, going to the movies, and my weakness, shopping.

In order to pay for my expensive taste, I had to have a source of income. Being a very involved student — socially, educationally, and athletically — I didn't have time for a full-time job. Most of my time was dominated by practicing with the swim team. Nonetheless, this turned out to my advantage. I found a job working at the pool where I practice teaching children to do what I know best — swimming. Not only was it convenient, and I was well-trained, but it turned out to be a great experience. I was earning money and developing my skills as a leader.

Though my income problems were solved, there was still the issue of managing my money. As an Internet-savvy student, I was delighted to know my bank provided an online banking site. This site helped me manage my finances more than anything else. I quickly figured out how to set a budget and track my spending. I saved all of my receipts, wrote everything in my transaction register, and once a week, I would balance it all online. (It conveniently fit in with my social time on Twitter and Facebook.) I saw how much I spent and how much I needed to spend. This taught me important lessons on budgeting my money and learning to work around my expensive taste.

However, as time went on, I got lazy. I lost a few receipts here and there, and fell behind in my transaction register. I put off balancing my checkbook. This carelessness proved to be a lifelong lesson.

When I finally decided it was time for me to check my online account again, I found out that I had overdrawn my account. I was devastated. How could I have let something like this happen? I could have prevented it by simply keeping track of my spending. I learned an important lesson, however. Overdrawing my bank account cost me $110. Never again will I let something so big happen that can be prevented by something so little.

Since then, I have regained control of my finances. I now keep careful track of everything I buy and earn. I will not let my account get overdrawn again. Managing my finances has not only taught me how to deal appropriately with money, but it has also taught me responsibility. If my parents had let me continue to "charge it" to their credit card, I would never know how to take care of myself in the real world. It was a tough pill to swallow, but now that I've got the hang of taking care of my money, I can face my future.

Here, become an adult

You've spent a lot of time under your parents' supervision. You've had to listen to their rules, and you've had to get their permission to do certain things. While it isn't necessarily bad to have parents watching over you, you are probably eager to be an adult and to make your own decisions. When you're an older teenager or college student, it's your turn to start making your own decisions after years of having other people telling you what to do.

Guess what? Credit card companies and other lenders know that you want to make your own decisions, and they also know that you may not have a full understanding of personal finance in order to know when to apply for credit and when not to. For this reason, some companies try to encourage young people to apply for credit as a form of asserting their independence. You will see marketing signs that promise a fun experience when you get your very own credit card. There may be pictures of young people smiling as they lug full bags of merchandise around. You might even see some images of young people enjoying things that many older adults don't even enjoy: a beautifully furnished apartment, a flashy car, or expensive dinners out. You need to realize that adulthood doesn't automatically equal every material thing you want. That's not what adulthood is about. In fact, if you ask any adult if he or she owns all the things he or she wants to have, chances are that you will get a resounding "No!" for an answer.

Even though having your own credit card is something you generally only get to have when you are an adult, having a credit card does not make you an adult. In other words, don't fall for marketing tactics that try to make it seem like getting a credit card is the key to becoming an independent adult. The truth is, you will have a much more successful chance of gaining independence from your parents if you aren't saddled with debt from credit cards and loans. In fact, if you load up on debt as a teenager or college student, , you're only increasing your odds of someday winding back up in your parents' home because you can't afford to live on your own. Approximately 65 percent of college graduates return home after finishing a degree, according to the U.S. Census Bureau.

Here is a guarantee: You will enjoy your independent years as an adult a lot more if you aren't up to your ears in debt.

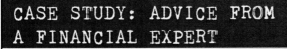

CASE STUDY: ADVICE FROM A FINANCIAL EXPERT

Andrew Housser - Co-CEO of Bills.com

Understand that your credit score is important, and a good score can significantly impact an individual's ability to borrow money as well as the interest rate they receive on this loan. Credit scores also can affect the ability to rent an apartment, lease a car, or even get a job.

When the time comes for a credit card, understand that it is only for convenience, not to extend buying ability. Never carry a balance; pay every bill on time and in full. Make sure to leave some room on credit cards. Do not "max out" accounts or charge up to the credit limit.

Understand the importance of building an emergency fund. Conventional wisdom holds that individuals need to save at least six months' worth of living expenses to prepare for the unexpected.

Learn the difference between healthy and unhealthy debt. Generally, only four types of debt can be healthy:

1. Student loans: Further one's education and increase future earning potential.
2. Mortgages: Home ownership is an asset that can build equity and net worth.
3. Necessary medical bills: One's health always takes priority.
4. Business debts: Often necessary to build a business and future earnings.

All other types of debt — especially credit card debt — create more problems than they solve.

Minimum payment: Bad news

You might wonder, "How can a credit card company make very much money off of me if I always make my payment on time?" It's great that you have every intention of making your payments on time every month, but even if you have a credit card that doesn't have monthly or annual usage fees, you are going to pay money in interest charges if you don't pay your balance in full each month. Don't forget: Credit card interest can build up quickly, leaving you with a much higher balance than you expected.

What is the minimum payment? This is the amount of money that the credit card company requires you to pay each month in order to avoid extra fees. In order to stay current with your account, you must pay at least the minimum payment requested by the lender. This amount can change from month to month based on how much money you owe. One month you might have a minimum payment of $40, and the next month you might have a minimum payment of $200; it all depends on your balance.

Did You Know?

Installment loans, like car loans, do not have varying minimum monthly payments. Your payment will be the same every month no matter what your balance is.

Lenders don't come up with minimum payments without a method. The minimum payment is based on a percentage of the balance you owe. The higher your balance, the higher your minimum monthly payment will be. That's why you can't assume that your payment will be the same from month to month — something to consider when you're working on your written budget.

Do you want to make a minimum monthly payment? The answer is yes, but you also want to pay more. Ideally, you should always pay off your balance every month to avoid interest charges, but if for some reason you can't manage the full balance payment one month, at least make the minimum monthly payment. This will keep you out of trouble with the lender. Keep in mind, though, that you should not make a habit of only making the minimum monthly payment. The minimum monthly payment will be too low of an amount to pay off the balance in any reasonable amount of time, especially when you consider that interest charges are constantly getting tagged on to the account balance.

Here is an example: Suppose you have a credit card balance of $500 with an interest rate of 18 percent. Your credit card company sets the minimum monthly payment at $20. You know that 500 divided by 20 is 25, so you might assume you will have the debt paid off in full in 25 months as long as you continue to make the minimum monthly payments. Never mind that you probably don't want to spend the next 25 months paying off a debt; you should know that if you make the monthly minimum payment every month, you're going to wind up paying it off in approximately 43 months — not 25.

How does 25 months turn into 43 months? It's all about interest. Do you remember reading in Chapter 3 about the how compound interest can make your savings account grow a lot faster than if you didn't earn any interest at all? The same principal applies to interest charged on your balance; however, in this case, the money earned goes straight to your credit card company. In other words, while interest is a great thing to have in your savings account, it is not such a great thing when it comes to owing money. In fact, if you make the minimum payment using the same numbers above, you will wind up paying almost $175 in interest payments by the time you get the balance paid off. What this really means is you paid the credit card company $175 to let you borrow $500. If your interest rate is higher, you'll wind up paying even more. For example, if your interest rate is 21 percent instead of 18 percent, it will take you an extra three months to pay off the balance and you'll pay just under $220 in interest charges. If it seems unfair to you to pay $220 in interest charges to borrow $500, keep in mind that you can avoid this completely by paying off your credit card debt in full every month. If you can't pay it off in full every month, at least make a larger payment than the minimum requested by the credit card company. This will help you to pay off the debt faster. The more money you put toward the balance you owe, the quicker it will get paid off, and the less interest you will wind up paying.

CASE STUDY: WORKING WHILE IN SCHOOL
Alexandra — High School Student

Managing my own personal finances has been something I have greatly cared about over the years. When I was 10 years old, my parents divorced. My father does not pay a lot of child support money toward me and my two sisters. Up until two years ago, when my mother remarried, my mother had basically supported us on her own. She has worked very hard to try and give us as comfortable a life as possible. Money for college, however, is another subject entirely. My father spent my college fund money. Thousands of thousands of dollars are gone. Because of this, I have since saved and spent my money wisely.

I work as a blackjack dealer for Casino Party Planners. My mother never wanted me to get a job after school because she was afraid it would interfere with my studies. As I am in the rigorous International Baccalaureate program, my studies are of the upmost importance. However, I still wanted to get a job on weekends that would pay for some of my expenses. With the money I earned, I was able to pay for half of my small, fuel-efficient car. The money I make is also used to put gas in my car twice a week. The rest of that money goes into my savings account, which I established when I was a sophomore. Besides working to earn money for my expenses now and my future college expenses, I also participate in fundraising efforts.

I am president of the Pink Ladies Service Club. The club gives out scholarships at the end of each year. We have three car washes annually to raise money for student scholarships. I have worked hard this year to fundraise in the hopes of being a recipient of one of those scholarships. If I am awarded it, the money I obtain will be put to the use of textbooks and housing, which is another money saver I could use.

What every freshman in college wants to have is an apartment. Unfortunately, I will not be one of those students. I did the smart, cost-efficient thing and signed up for a dorm. The dorm will hopefully be in the Honors

Hall at Florida State University, where I will be attending school in their Honors program. By applying for a double dorm, I have saved a lot of money than by renting an apartment by myself.

2008 was not a good year for business for my mother and step-father. My mother is the broker of her own real estate company and my step-father is the other realtor in the business. The real estate market was in a downward spiral this past year. This is why I am trying to obtain as much scholarship money as possible. I would like to make the financial burden of college as little as possible for my mother. That is why I try so hard to save financially.

What if I don't pay?

If you are new to credit, you may not fully understand the importance of paying on time, every time. Make no mistake about it; creditors are serious when they set a due date. It isn't just a suggestion that you get money to them by a certain date — it's a must.

Some lenders offer a grace period for the payment, which means even though your due date has been set to a specific date, they won't consider the payment late until after the grace period. For example, suppose your credit card account due date is listed as the 5th of the month, but the lender offers a ten-day grace period. This means that as long as you get the payment to the lender by the 15th, you won't run into any late payment fees or negative marks on your account.

Keep in mind, though, that some creditors don't offer generous grace periods. You should never assume you have a grace period unless you know for sure. Even if you have a grace period, try to make your payment before the actual due date; you never really know what could happen. A problem with the mail or an electronic hiccup on a website might make your payment late. It is better to get into the habit now of making payments quickly instead of waiting until the last minute. When you're older and have more bills, waiting until the last minute to pay can result in missed payments and mistakes.

Here is a sample timeline of what can happen when you don't make your credit card or loan payments on time:

1. If your payment does not arrive by the due date, your creditor will probably contact you to let you know that you are due. Some creditors will contact you before the grace period (if you have one) runs out to give you the chance to make your payment prior to any late fees, but not all creditors will bother. Most would rather you incur as many fees as possible. If you're contacted, it will probably be by telephone or e-mail. If creditors contact you by telephone, you may get an automated recording telling you to please call to discuss your account.

   If you contact the creditor before the grace period is up, you will probably be given the chance to make a payment the same day, either over the phone or online. For a same day payment, the creditor will ask permission to withdraw money directly from your bank account. There is usually a fee that comes with making a same day payment, and sometimes the fee can be high, approximately $15 to $25. That's a small price to pay for keeping your account current, and hopefully, you will learn your lesson the first time and never have to deal with this hefty fee again. After all, there are some adults who pay these large fees all the time just because they can't seem to keep up with their due dates. Avoid this habit, and you'll save quite a bit of money.

The day the late fee shows up on your account depends on the policies of the credit card company. A late fee will show up quicker on an account with no grace period than on an account with one. For this reason, a late fee might occur the day after your payment's due date if no payment was received, or might be delayed until after the grace period. You may also find that the late fee doesn't show up on your account until the next statement cycle. If you want to know the specific date a late fee will be assessed on your credit card statement, talk to a representative at your credit card company.

Safety first!

Just because someone calls to talk to you about your account does not mean this person actually works for your creditor. Always ask to make sure who you are speaking with. If they ask you security questions, answer one slightly wrong to see if they correct you.

2. If you ignore the requests for payment from your creditor, your account goes into delinquent status. This means that you are no longer considered to have a current account and you are officially behind in paying your bill. Many different things can happen at this point, depending on how you react to the situation and what the procedures are with your lender.

    •   You might be able to pay the bill and have any late fee reversed if you call the company and talk to a representative, explaining why you were late with your payment. This usually only works if you already have a long history of making payments on time and your creditor allows for fee reversals (not every company will reverse fees, even if there is a really great excuse for the late payment). If you do bring the account current and get the late fee reversed, you may still wind up with other problems, which are mentioned below.

- Your creditor may raise your interest rate as a result of your late payment. Suppose you opened the account at a really low, impressive interest rate. When you miss a payment, you run the risk of getting assigned what is called the default interest rate. This is the high interest rate that the creditor assigns to accounts that fall into default by being late or otherwise not following the original credit agreement. Remember: When you don't pay your debts on time, you're essentially breaking a promise to the creditor. When you sign a store receipt for a purchase with a credit card, the signature line usually states "I promise to pay this amount in accordance with my card member agreement." When you sign this, you're entering into a contract. Break the terms of the contract and the creditor is allowed to raise your interest rate, charge you fees, and do anything else that is listed in the original agreement you signed when you first opened the account.

Did You Know?

Does this all sound complicated? You can avoid dealing with all of this by always making your payments on time.

- When your account becomes 30 days overdue, your creditor may list it as delinquent on your credit report. Rest assured that you don't want an account listed as delinquent on your credit report — this will make you a much less desirable applicant for years to come.

3. If you continue to ignore the requests for payment, your creditor will get a little more aggressive in trying to get money from you. You will start getting phone calls from collectors, and you will get letters in the mail that are designed to make you panic about making your payment. As you keep ignoring the requests, chances are good that your creditor is adding plenty of fees to your account. Guess what? You will also pay interest on all of those fees.

You should know that while collection agents can sometimes be aggressive and somewhat gruff, they *do not* have the right to be abusive to you or to threaten you in any way, such as calling you a deadbeat for not paying your bill or wondering aloud if they should come to your house to collect from you face to face. They also aren't allowed to share information about your debt to anyone else who is not listed as a signer on the account .This means they aren't allowed to tell your parents how much you owe on the account if you parents are not listed as a signer and if your parents are no longer legally responsible for your ac-

tions. If you are away at college, and a collector calls your mom and tells her all about your delinquent account that she is not a signer for, that collector has broken the law. The bottom line is that while you do owe money to a collector, and you should pay that money back, it does not give a collector the right to be verbally abusive to you or to try to get someone else in your family to pay your debt if that family member is not a signer on your account.

4. If you still don't pay what you owe, depending on what type of debt it is, you may wind up being sued by the lender, or you may get the item you purchased with the credit taken away — an act called repossession. For example, if the account is a car loan or another loan used to finance the purchase of something, the lender can take that item back. The timeframe for things like this vary according to the lender, but you may find that in the case of a car loan, all it takes is missing three or four payments before the lender repossesses the car from you. Make no mistake about it; you cannot charge a bunch of purchases and just ignore the payments that are due. There are consequences to your financial actions

5. If several months go by (usually over 180 days) and you still don't pay the debt, your creditor may just decide to give up, and the account will go into charge-off status. This means the creditor does not plan on pursuing you for payment anymore, but this does not mean you are no longer financially responsible for the debt. The account will be listed on your credit report as a charge-off, which never looks good to future potential lenders and drags

your credit score down quite a bit depending on what else is already listed on your credit report. When this happens, sometimes collection agencies purchase bad debt from lenders. When doing this, they pay a portion of the amount you owe to the original lender and then the debt legally becomes theirs to collect. For example, suppose you have an Old Navy credit card and you stop making payments on debt owed to the store. Old Navy tries for months to get you to pay your bill with no success. Old Navy then decides to no longer chase you in an attempt to get you to pay. A collection agency comes along and purchases the account from Old Navy. Now, instead of Old Navy asking for payment, you will begin to receive letters and phone calls from this collection agency, which now has the legal right to pursue you for the money. So, even if the original lender gives up on getting the money from you, don't assume you won't eventually have to pay the money back to someone else.

If you reach this stage, don't be surprised if your debt has grown quite a bit. When you ignore your debts, your debt begins to accrue fees while also increasing with the default interest rate. You may start out with a relatively small debt of $400, but by the time the collection agency contacts you to collect payment, your debt has grown closer to $1000 due to the fees, penalties, and interest that has piled up on the debt while you've been ignoring it.

Do you really want to wind up in a situation like this? Wouldn't it be much easier to just make your payments on time or, better yet, not max out your credit cards in the first place? People who get into trouble with credit do so because they don't look at the bigger picture. They don't realize that a small debt can wind up turning into a huge debt when it isn't paid on time, and they also underestimate the hassle that can come with dealing with collectors who call several times a day in an attempt to get their money back. If you think your parents calling you to check on you is annoying, imagine a collector calling three or four times a day to demand money from you. It isn't fun.

CASE STUDY: REPAIRING YOUR CREDIT SCORE

Excerpt from "How to Repair Your Credit Score Now: Simple No Cost Methods You Can Put to Use Today" By Jamaine Burrell

"Debt provides a method of taking advantage of opportunities and experiences that enhance the quality of one's life and provide enjoyment and fulfillment. Homes, vehicles, vacations, education, and all of the things that enhance one's quality of life are obtainable by making good use of debt.

Good use of debt requires that one develop a spending plan that incorporates methods of properly maintaining and managing the acquired debt. Almost everyone will rely upon credit at some point. Whether credit is used to finance luxury and big ticket items, such as a car, or it is used to finance an unexpected medical or other emergency, one needs to be put in the position of being capable of acquiring the necessary financing when it is needed or wanted.

By borrowing responsibly, one builds a positive credit history that indicates to lenders that they are a good risk for lending money. Most lenders examine one's past history of using credit in determining whether to issue additional credit. If one's credit history indicates a commitment to managing debt properly, the lender is more likely to extend the necessary financing when needed and also provide the most favorable interest rates and payment schedule."

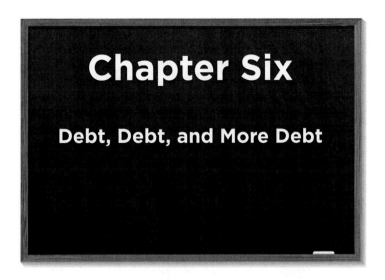

Chapter Six

Debt, Debt, and More Debt

If you live in mainstream society, chances are good you will, at some point, wind up with some form of debt. Whether you wind up with a wallet stuffed full of credit cards or a mortgage loan to purchase your own house, there are very few people who avoid debt altogether. Debt does not have to be a bad thing, but if you aren't careful, it will take control of your life.

Have you ever experienced the feeling that comes along with owing someone money? Suppose you owe your friend $20. Imagine every time you see that friend he says, "Hey! Where is my $20?" Pretty soon he says, "You know that $20 you owed me? Well now you owe me $25 because you didn't pay me quickly enough." Later, if you still haven't paid him back, he says, "Because you haven't paid me back yet, I'm going to talk to everyone who might want to lend you money and tell them to stay away from you because you don't pay your debts back fast enough." Then, when you do finally pay the debt back, he turns around and says, "Would you like to borrow $30 this time?" This is similar to how credit works. As long as you owe a lender money, the lender is going to pursue payment. If you don't pay the money back like you should, the lender is going to tell other lenders (through your credit report) they shouldn't lend money to you. Then, when you do pay the lender, you might find the lender is suddenly willing to lend you more money. It's a perpetual cycle, and it only ends if you make the conscious effort to end it.

CASE STUDY: EARNING YOUR OWN WAY

Mary — High School Student

Ever since I was 14 years old, I have had to pay for everything by myself, without my mom's help. On my 14th birthday, my mom hired me to work for her. She purchased a laptop for me — shortly after I started high school — so I can use it for my school work; her condition was that I pay her back for it. Every month I pay her a certain amount of money, I will continue to do that until I have paid her the correct amount.

I receive my paychecks through direct deposit from my work. It goes straight into my bank account, which I access online. That is how I pay my mom back each month. I use my debit card when I need to spend money. I only spend money when I absolutely have to. I keep my debit card in my mom's desk so I'm not tempted to spend money. I am saving my money so I can buy a car when I turn 16, or shortly afterwards, and also so I can pay for college.

I often have to convince myself that I can't spend money, because I have to save it, but sometimes it isn't easy. Because my mom doesn't pay for anything, I have to buy myself everything that I want. If I need clothes for the new school year, I have to buy them; if I want to go out with friends, I have to pay for it; if I need school supplies or anything else, I have to pay for it. I have to keep track of how much money I have, which I do both online and in my checkbook. Every time I spend money using my debit card, my bank automatically puts $1 into savings, which helps me save money.

Good Debt and Bad Debt

Financial experts put debt into one of two categories: good debt and bad debt. Don't be fooled into thinking that just because something is called good debt that it doesn't mean you have to pay it back. Good and bad just refers to what you are getting out of the things you buy with the debt.

Good debt

Good debt refers to debt that was used for purchases that have the potential to grow your wealth over time. For example, a mortgage loan used to purchase a house is considered good debt because houses hopefully appreciate in value over time. When a house appreciates in value, it means that a house purchased for $200,000 may be worth $210,000 in a year. In theory, people are supposed to be able to purchase a home with a mortgage for a certain amount and then be able to sell the home for more money than they originally spent, thus increasing their wealth. This isn't always the case, but debt from buying a home is still considered to be good debt.

Student loans also fall into the category of good debt because they are considered to be a way to finance your education, thereby investing in your future. Keep in mind that just because something falls into the category of good debt does not mean you should aspire to obtain as much of it as you can. Good debt has to be paid back, just like bad debt.

Bad debt

Some people will argue that all debt is bad, no matter what it is labeled, but there are some debts that are always considered bad. In other words, you should avoid this type of debt if at all possible because it will do nothing to make you wealthier in the long run. Credit cards, car loans, and other types of loans that aren't for housing or college expenses fall into the category of bad debt.

When trying to figure out if a debt is good or bad, think about how the debt will affect your overall finances. Ask yourself these questions:

- **Does this item help me make more money in the long run?** A student loan may someday pay off because a college degree may help you to make more money in the future, but a shopping spree for clothing using a credit card will only hurt your finances.

- **Will my purchase appreciate in value?** When something appreciates, it means that the item becomes worth more over time. A home may appreciate in value, making a mortgage loan a good debt, but a car will probably depreciate (lose value) over time, making it a bad debt.

- **Does it really matter if it is good or bad debt?** Putting your debt into one category or another does not mean you won't have to pay the debt back with interest. The more debt you can avoid, the better your finances will be.

While it is true you may never be able to afford to buy a house in cash, almost everything else can probably be obtained using the tried and true method of saving for what you want. Are there people out there who buy cars with cash and who pay for their entire college education without ever taking out a single loan? There certainly are, although these people have learned the important talent of working toward what they want and delaying their gratification. They have spent a long time saving money and have set clear plans to achieve their financial goals.

CASE STUDY: THE IMPORTANCE OF SAVING
Michelle – High School Student

One thing kids today don't realize is that saving for life after high school is very important. I have started to save for college recently, though I don't have as much money set aside as I probably should. However, I am applying for many scholarships, and I hope that through these, I will be able to gain more money to pay for books and transportation. In the state of Florida, the Bright Futures Scholarship Program is also offered, and I qualify for it, so at the present time I do not need to worry too much about tuition as I am commuting to a community college during my first two years. I have been told this is a good idea to follow because I will not only avoid paying tuition, but I won't have to pay for dorm and food expenses.

I have realized that, even if I didn't plan on going to college, it's still important to save money throughout and after high school. Though I could plan to go directly into the workforce after graduating, money saved can serve as a backup for any sort of emergency. Your job may be fine one day, and then layoffs are conducted a week later. I could get sick, and if I have no medical insurance, I would have quite an expense to worry about. In either circumstance, I believe it's vital to start saving money whenever I can for whatever the situation calls for.

I have also learned how to manage household bills over the last year and a half, which helps me to see the importance of money management. I learned I not only need to have enough money saved on my own to take care of everyday things and emergencies, but I also must have a sufficient amount of money to cover my expenses. Sometimes, it doesn't seem easy, but once a system is worked out, I have seen it's actually something that's very simple to do — if you have the means to do it.

On a final note, I have come to see that if I can learn to save money now, I can practice discipline when it comes to spending. This is a trait that will carry over with me into the future and will help me to manage my money in an even better fashion. If other students will practice this now,

> many of them will see they don't have to struggle as much in order to make it through college or their first few years out of high school. All it takes is a little practice and a lot of patience.

Handle your debt

If you are going to have debt, you will need to learn how to handle it. Here are some basic rules to follow regarding your debt:

- **Don't get credit you don't need**. It is one thing to get a loan to pay for college when you don't have any other way to pay for your education, but it is another thing entirely to get a credit card from your favorite store in the mall so you can buy clothes whenever you want. Before you obtain credit, think about whether you really need the things you are about to finance. While there are important expenses in life such as tuition and rent, using credit unnecessarily should be avoided.

- **Don't view available balances as invitations to splurge**. Credit card companies would like nothing more than for you to charge your credit card accounts to the maximum limit because it makes more money for them in the long run due to fees and interest charges. It will also make it more difficult for you to manage your finances, and you will probably find yourself psychologically affected by the debt. Don't make the mistake of thinking that owing a large sum of money won't bother you, because it will.

- **Don't hoard credit**. You may like the idea of getting credit in your own name, and while this can indeed be something that makes you feel more independent, it is also something that can get you into a lot of trouble. Remember that just because a creditor is willing to give you a loan or credit card does not mean they know you can actually afford the payments. For this reason, avoid the temptation to apply for every credit card you're offered, especially when shopping at the mall or at department stores.

- **Keep track of your debt.** Being unable to pay off your balances in full every month should be a huge red flag to you, warning you that you have too much debt. While trying to pay off the balances you have, always keep track of how much you owe along with when the payments are due. The last thing you want to do is to fall behind in your payments and wind up being harassed by collection agencies all day long.

- **Don't forget to save.** If you find yourself scrambling to pay off the debt, you might be tempted to drain out your savings account or stop saving altogether. Use caution. You need some money in savings to handle any financial emergencies that might come up. What will you do if your car breaks down and you don't have any money left in your savings account to pay for the repairs? Chances are you will use a credit card to cover the repairs, and this starts the whole debt cycle over again.

- **Don't rely on credit.** If you find you are using credit in order to cover basic expenses, such as for groceries or to pay utility bills, you are already in trouble financially. Scale back your spending to allow you to pay for everything in cash while getting your debt under control.

How do you get your debt under control? It can be an easy pro-cess if you haven't yet fallen too deeply into debt, and it can be a really tough process if you're in serious financial trouble. Either way, the effort is really worth the end result, and the sooner you get started, the more quickly you can start to actually enjoy your money instead of seeing it as nothing more than a way to pay off the debt you owe.

Why should you bother to learn about getting out of debt if you aren't even old enough to get credit on your own? The fact is that you never know what the future will hold, so learning about these methods now will prepare you for when you are older and may find yourself in a situation where you need to turn your finances around. Better yet, maybe reading about debt will keep you from ever getting in too deep to begin with.

Keep in mind that you don't have to use credit if you don't want to. There are people who live without any debt at all. Do you remember the story from Chapter 1 about the man who gave up money altogether? If a man can give up using any form of money whatsoever, it doesn't seem so far-fetched to think you can live without incurring debt.

CASE STUDY: YOUR FIRST CAR

Margaret – High School Student

Every 16-year-old has the dream of their perfect car. For me, it was a lime green Volkswagen. I wanted this car ever since I was a little girl. So, naturally, I almost died when my mother gave me my dream car on my birthday. Little did I know, this car would put me in financial, emotional, and mental agony.

My mother surprised me with me car on a Friday after school. She told me earlier that morning that we were going to go car shopping after school, but what I didn't know is she had already struck a deal with the dealer. I was so happy and sad at the same time. Not only did this mean I was growing up, but it also meant I had a responsibility — car payments. We didn't have enough to pay off the car, and insurance payments were now in my future.

At the time, I didn't have a job, so all the payment issues were on the shoulders of my mother. I did little odd jobs like babysitting to help pay all the expenses, but we were still behind. With all these problems, you would think we already had enough on our plate, but the story just gets better and better. My precious car was experiencing some mechanical difficulties that would make it almost impossible to drive — problems the dealer claimed were not his problem now that we had exceeded the warranty. We went to every car repair shop in town. Time and money seemed to vanish right in front of our eyes as we went to every pointless car repair. It seemed there was no hope in sight for our little bundle of chaos. Our last resort was to take the car to a foreign car dealership and see if there was anything they could do. Of course, in the back of my mind, I knew that it was going to cost an arm and a leg to fix — an arm and a leg I didn't have.

"The problem is in the computer's memory within the car," the repair man said. You can imagine the look on our faces. I had never heard of a car having a computer within it. To repair it would cost too much, and who's to say that this problem won't happen again? I was able to trade it in for a wonderful car that is better on payments and (knock on wood) hasn't given me any trouble since I bought it.

I know that if it wasn't for me making reasonable and logical decisions, I would still have that money-munching vehicle. I am satisfied with my decision, and happy my mother was able to help me along the way. My advice to teens buying used cars: Always look into what you are purchasing. Always make sure that you are financially stable enough to be able to handle whatever life hands you.

People who live without credit have to live within their means, which basically means they just don't buy things they can't afford. Instead of pulling out a credit card to pay for a trip to the mall, these people pay with cash or just stay out of the mall to begin with. If they don't have the money to buy something, they just don't buy it. The funny thing about this lifestyle is that oftentimes, these people find they have more than enough money for everything they need. Why? It is because their money stays in their wallets or savings account instead of being used to pay credit card and loan payments.

If you avoid credit and debt altogether, you may run into a few issues that will complicate things just a little. For example, when you try to reserve a rental car or hotel room, most companies want a credit card to make the reservation. Some companies will accept a debit card for reservations, but they may put a hold on a large chunk of your money in your account until you pay the final bill. That means that if the company insists on putting a $500 hold on your checking account, you won't have access to that $500 until after you are finished with the car rental, hotel stay, or whatever it is you paid for. If you have the money available for a hold of this amount, it won't be a problem for you, but if you aren't expecting a hold like this, it can be a rude surprise.

You might also run into small problems when you apply for a job, insurance, or to rent an apartment. In all of these situations, your credit might be checked, and if you don't have any sort of credit history at all, you may have to show that you're able to pay your bills in other ways. You may be able to show copies of other bills you have paid, such as your cell phone bill or your cable bill, to prove that you are able to make your payments on time before you can get approved to rent an apartment from a landlord who only allows renters with a good credit history.

$ave $mart Tip

"Save as much as possible for college, and apply for every scholarship and contest that you possibly can. It is possible to win enough to actually pay for college and put extra in the bank."

Debra Lipphardt, scholarship coordinator and author of *The Scholarship and Financial Aid Solution: How to Go to College for Next to Nothing with Short Cuts, Tricks, and Tips from Start to Finish REVISED 2ND EDITION.*

You don't *need* credit, but it does make things easier if you can maintain a good payment history. The trick is to manage your credit well so that it doesn't become a problem. If you decide to live without credit, even if it's only in the beginning of your adult life, here's how to do it:

1. **Have ample savings**. Lots of people use their credit cards for financial emergencies, but if you don't plan to have credit cards, you need to have money stashed away in case something happens. Suppose you are away from home for

your first year of college and one of your family members has been injured in a car accident. You want to fly home and see that person, but if you don't have a credit card to buy the ticket and don't have any money available in your bank account, you will be out of luck. A portion of your paycheck should be put into a savings account to accommodate such emergencies.

2. **Keep records of your payments**. Because eventually you will need to prove to someone that you know how to make payments on time (like when you try to rent an apartment, for example), you should always keep detailed records. Hold on to your statements and receipts for any bills that you pay monthly, such as rent from the place where you live now (if you pay rent) or car insurance. If you don't have monthly bills, you may need to get reference letters written by someone who you have paid a debt to; however, some potential landlords and other people won't accept something like this as proof of good payment history. As you can see, credit is sometimes a necessary evil. You will likely wind up with some sort of credit eventually, and when you do, the trick is to learn how to manage it effectively.

3. **Get ready to explain yourself**. Suppose you go for ten years without obtaining any credit whatsoever, and then you decide that the time has come to get a loan so you can buy a house. When you submit an application for your mortgage loan, chances are good the lender will contact you and want an explanation as to why you have no credit history. During your late teens or early 20s, not having a credit history is expected. However, by the time you are in

your late 20s or early 30s, lenders expect for you to have established some sort of credit history. If you manage to get to this point without using credit, you will definitely shock most lenders, and you may have a difficult time buying the house. With a large amount of savings, it is entirely possible to get approved for a mortgage loan without having a credit history, but it will be a lot harder than if you obtained credit and used it wisely before applying for the home loan.

Most likely, you will eventually get a credit card or obtain some other form of credit, whether it is a car loan or a mortgage. Credit cards, when used responsibly and when only used when you have the money to pay off the balance each month, don't have to be a negative thing. Some people, however, lack the self-control to only spend what they can afford to pay, and that is how many people get in trouble with credit cards. So, if you do eventually get a credit card, remember to pay your bills on time and try to pay off the balance of the card each month. If that's not possible because you have had to use the card for an emergency, pay off the balance as quickly as possible and try to pay more than the minimum payment each month to avoid paying a lot of interest.

CASE STUDY: CREATIVE WAYS TO GET BY

Gary – College Student

I pretty much got cut off by my father's checkbook for dating a girl. Being young and arrogant, I told him I didn't need his money when it would have just been smarter to hide my girlfriend until I had my college paid for. Anyway, my girlfriend, Amy, and I survived and were pretty clever at getting things for nothing.

Food:
I took a job at the university's cafeteria. It didn't really pay anything, but for washing dishes for an hour a day, I got free meals at the cafeteria.

Amy took a job at a convenience store. When they had supplies that were about to hit their expiration date, the manager would sign them off, and Amy was permitted to take them home. Milk actually can last after the date if unopened. We used it up quickly, but for free, it was worth it.

Entertainment:
I had a friend who was a bouncer for a Cincinnati concert arena. Because our school was about two hours away, he made a deal with me that if I did the driving to and from the concert, he would get me into them for free. I got in through the security gate and got free concerts for two summers. It also helped to have a friend who worked the local movie theater. I tutored her in math, and she got us into the movies for free. Also, I was taking theater courses which required that we attend the university plays for analysis and discussions, and the good part was that we got free tickets for them.

Rent:
Because we did not go home for the summer when school was out, we had a deal with the landlord to keep an eye on things (parties and such), so we got discounted rent during the summer months. Plus, when college kids left for the summer, a lot of their furniture and such was being thrown out. We pretty much had a really stocked apartment and didn't pay for any of it.

College:
Helping as a lab assistant worked well to get access to computers, copier machines, and other equipment I needed but could not afford.

All in all, I lived by using improvisation skills and fast-talking to get away with it.

The debt spiral

It is really easy to get into trouble with debt. Even if you manage to keep up on all your payments, you might find yourself overwhelmed with the amount of money you owe. It can be frustrating to know a portion of your paycheck will go straight to a creditor instead of going into your savings account or toward buying something you really want.

The bright side to a frustrating situation with debt is there is always a way out. It may take you years to get your debt paid off, but with a conscious effort, eventually, it'll happen. You have to first recognize the fact that you are in financial trouble and decide you want to do something about it.

Debt may not be a huge problem for you now, especially if you have not yet entered college. College is when many people first experience financial difficulties, not only because of the financial obligations associated with attending college, but also because this may be the first time you have some control over your finances.

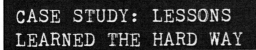

CASE STUDY: LESSONS
LEARNED THE HARD WAY

Chris – College Graduate

I spent myself into a frenzy when I was in college. I spent so much money that I graduated with a car-sized student debt going to state schools. I did it in part to live like the kids I hung out with. I wanted to go home for the holidays. I didn't want to work full-time and go to school full-time. This makes perfect sense given I was from a cash-strapped family. Education was important, recreation was desirable, and resources were available.

I racked up a bunch of debt and then stopped paying for it. I couldn't possibly afford my private debt. The only reason I started paying back my student loans is because creditors finally got serious. My student loans are back on deferment as of now. My credit has been ruined.

We were taught to create debt. We have created debt, and in doing so, we have taught our children to create debt. But debt usually has a creditor. In the United States, we have historically had much more liberty from harassment and mistreatment by creditors than in most other countries. Still, they have some options available to them.

But more important than the threat of a repo man is the empty fulfillment offered by the accumulation of debt and stuff. Everything I like to do costs money. Everyone I love costs money. This is not because I am money-hungry, nor are those I care about. These are problems because money is a lens through which all of the light of the world passes.

Are you in trouble?

If you're still in high school, you are probably wondering why this is important to you. The best time to learn about how to get out of debt is before you're actually in it. Learning about debt now may stop you from ever getting into trouble with debt in the first place.

Chances are, if you're having trouble with debt, you'll know it. While it is certainly true that mounding debt seems to sneak up on people when they first begin using credit, it is not difficult to realize when things begin to get out of control. Here are some of the signs that you are heading toward trouble with debt:

- You can no longer pay off the full balance of your credit card each month.

- You use credit cards to buy necessities like food or gas because you can't afford to pay for them with cash.
- You have no idea how much money you owe or when your payments are due.
- You have to borrow money from other people to make all your debt payments.
- You start missing payment due dates.
- Your credit applications get turned down for reasons other than lack of credit history.
- You have creditors trying to contact you because you are behind on payments.
- You feel anxious or depressed because of your financial situation.

This last sign is important. No matter how effectively you manage your bills and how careful you are about making your payments, the second you start to feel uncomfortable about how much money you owe to creditors, it is time to make some changes. Trust your instincts. If it starts to feel like you are losing control of your money, you probably are.

CASE STUDY: AMASSED STUDENT LOANS

Josh — College Graduate

I amassed $40,000 in student loans over the course of four years in college while pursuing a degree in filmmaking. I worked about 25 hours a week as a salesman at a department store, and my pay wasn't enough to live on. The student loans covered my college tuition, books, and living expenses such as rent. The last year of school, I had a car loan, so some student loan money went to pay that, too.

Looking back, it might have been too easy to get the large amount of money from student loans. In retrospect, if I had more self-discipline, I would have borrowed less from student loans because, really, I didn't need it all. I could have found a job that paid more and been more frugal, but it was just so easy to get the money from the student loans.

About six months or a year after graduating from college, the student loan payments started, and I paid them off and on. I then went on a payment plan with the loan creditor for awhile, where payments were automatically taken out of my checking account, but it wasn't a mandatory program; it wasn't like they were garnishing my account or anything. After two or three instances of having insufficient funds when the withdrawal was attempted, they took me off the automatic payments. After that I was supposed to start paying them on my own, but I haven't yet. This was about two years ago, and I'm not paying on them now because I'm out of work.

I wasn't paying on them before because I didn't think I had the money to spare, but I'm not paying on them now because I know I don't have the money as I am not working. When tax time rolls along, there is a tax lien on any return due to me; so last year, my whole tax return went to the student loans. I was due a tax return, but I never saw any of it.

Frankly, I stopped keeping track of the late fees and penalties that have been added to the student loan accounts because I know I don't have the money to pay it, so there is nothing I can really do about it at this point. I would guess the penalties and fees have added up to around $3,000 or more.

I have some advice for college students who are thinking about getting student loans to help pay for college: Get as little money as you possibly can. Get just what you need, and nothing more. There were times when I wasn't working too much in college, so I pretty much relied on the student loan money to pay all my living expenses, which was a huge mistake. Try not to use the funds for anything except expenses directly related to college, like tuition and books.

Getting rid of debt

There are many different ways to pay off debt. The best way to pay down debt is whatever method works best for you. There are many different financial experts who claim their ideas for paying off debt are better than anyone else's, but unless the plan works with your situation, you will likely be unable to stick with the system.

Keep in mind that this is something you may not have to deal with right now at all. You may not even be at an age where you can obtain debt on your own. For this reason, this book only presents a brief review of the two most popular ways to systematically pay off debt. The important thing to learn right now is that there are methods to help you pay off debt, and if you sit by idly, dwelling on your woes rather than working to better them, you'll likely be in debt for the rest of your life. Remember this in few years if you find yourself in a financial situation you aren't prepared to handle on your own.

Debt laddering: Climb on down!

Debt laddering is a method used to pay down debt when you have more than one credit account. Here is how it works:

1. Look at all your credit accounts and figure out which one has the highest interest rate charged on the account. You can find the interest rate by examining your monthly statements. This is the card you should work to pay off first. Payments sent to this card should be substantially more than the minimum payment. You should pay the minimum monthly payment on all your other accounts,

while the account with the highest interest rate should get as much extra money as possible.

2. When the account with the highest interest rate is fully paid off, move on to the next account with the highest interest rate. Do the same thing with this account: Put as much extra money toward the balance as you can and only pay the minimum monthly payment on all the other accounts. In order for this method to be effective in getting you out of debt, the financial experts who endorse this method suggest the accounts should be closed after you pay them off.

3. Each time an account is paid off, move on to the next remaining account with the highest interest rate. The point is to keep doing this until all the accounts are paid off.

This method will only work quickly if you stop using the accounts you are trying to pay off; otherwise, you will spend more time paying off your balances because you keep adding to them.

Debt snowball: Watch it melt!

The debt snowball method is similar to the debt-laddering method, but with one small difference. Instead of starting with the credit account with the highest interest rate, you start with the account with the smallest balance and go from there.

This method may not make as much sense mathematically as the debt-laddering method because you will probably wind up paying more money in the long run because of interest. However this method is said to be more gratifying because, in theory, you will pay off accounts quicker than with the debt-laddering method. The idea is that quickly paying off accounts will keep you motivated and make you want to keep working toward paying off all your debt instead of getting discouraged and giving up. After all, a huge part of managing your finances is psychological. If you can talk yourself into getting serious about paying down your debt, you will have a better chance of succeeding with your goal than if you only worked toward it half-heartedly.

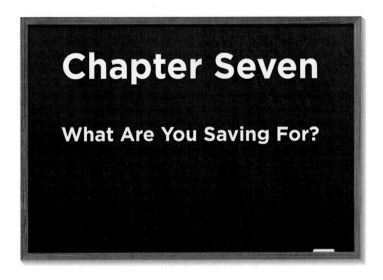

Chapter Seven

What Are You Saving For?

You probably hear it all the time: "Save your money! Stash some money away for a rainy day! Don't forget to save!" In fact, you've heard it throughout this book. You might feel like all the adults around you are entirely too alarmist when it comes to money and there really is not such a need to save so much money. You might think to yourself, "If I need money for something, I'll just go out and earn some. Why bother putting money away if it's just going to sit there?"

It is an understandable perspective, but by now, you should know there are many different reasons why you should save money. Maybe you want to save for a big expense, like a car or college tuition, or maybe you just want to have money available because you know that financial emergencies can pop up any time. Whether you're saving for something fun, like a new computer or the ability to go on a mini shopping spree, or you're saving without a specific future purchase in mind, saving is an important aspect of becoming financially independent.

Did You Know?

Money sitting in a savings account is considered an asset and can help you someday get approved for a home loan, even if you don't use the money in your savings account to buy the house.

How to Save

You learned about deposit accounts in Chapter 3, so you already know there are plenty of different places you can stash your cash. In this chapter, you will examine the reasons for saving, as well as ways you can make sure you are saving enough for the goals you are trying to reach.

There is a difference between saving with a specific purchase in mind and saving just to have money available in case you eventually need it for something in the future. While both goals are important, you will use different tactics, depending on what you are saving for.

Saving for things you want to buy

Sometimes, it is a lot easier to save for specific purchases than it is to save for nothing in particular. There is something about having an eventual goal that makes it a little easier to stash money into a savings account instead of spending the money on fun stuff.

What are you saving for? Whether it is something as big as a car or something as small as tickets to a concert, figuring out how much money to save is simple because you have an idea of how much the purchase is going to cost. If you know you have three years before you will have your driver's license, and you really

want to purchase a car once you get your license, all it takes is some simple math to figure out how much money you should save each month to make it happen.

For example, suppose you know you want to buy a used car that will cost you approximately $4,000. You want to be able to pay for the car in cash, and you want to buy it as closely to your 16th birthday as possible. Figure out how many months you have until your 16th birthday, then figure out how much money you will need to save each month in order to reach your goal of $4,000. In the following example, suppose you are 13 years old and you want to figure out how much you need to save each month to reach the $4,000 goal; the equation would look like this:

Months you have until your 16th birthday: 32

Divide the amount of money you want to save by the months you have to save: $4,000/32 months = $125

In order to have $4,000 in time for your 16th birthday, you will need to save approximately $125 per month.

After doing the equation, you then have a few choices to make. Is it realistic for you to save $125 a month? If you have a monthly income, this may not be such a big deal, but if you have very little money coming in each month, you may not be able to scrape together that much money. If this is the case, you have a few different options. You can lower the amount of money you want to save for your car, or you can give yourself more time to save for your car and, instead, decide to buy your car on your 17th or 18th birthday. You can switch your plan and save for the down payment on your car instead of paying for it in full with cash. On the other hand, you can also decide to figure out a way to make more money every month by getting a job or asking for an increase in pay for the job you already have.

Don't forget: You will earn interest on the money you save for your goal as long as you put the money into a bank account that pays interest. You should also cut yourself some slack if you miss a month here or there. Saving can be tough when you have other expenses to cover, so it is understandable that sometimes it is not possible to put the same amount of money away every single month. Make up for this by adding extra to your savings account whenever you can and by not dipping into your savings account for things you really do not need. Who knows? You may actually be able to save more money than you anticipated and buy a nicer car, or put the extra money toward gas or car insurance.

Use the same method when saving for smaller expenses. Suppose you know a band is coming to your city, and tickets go on sale next month. You really want to go see the band, so to you it is worth it to put some money aside to make sure you can get great seats. In this instance, you might use a weekly equation instead of a monthly one:

Weeks you have until tickets go on sale: 4

Divide the cost of the ticket by the weeks you have until the tickets go on sale: $50/4 = $12.50

You will have to save $12.50 per week in order to buy the concert ticket in four weeks. $12.50 sure seems more reasonable than $50, doesn't it? By breaking the expense up into manageable chunks, you make it possible to buy the things you want without having to borrow money from anyone to pay for them.

CASE STUDY: PURCHASING A CAR

Hannah – High School Student

For as long as I can remember, my parents have always taught me that in life things are not just handed to you, and you have to work hard to fulfill dreams and goals. Even though at a young age I did not understand this, now I do, and I respect my parents for everything they taught me.

One of the most significant goals in my life is to purchase my own vehicle. Since I started driving, I have shared a vehicle with either my Mom or Dad. It is very difficult to do things and be where we need to be when someone else is using the van. I decided I needed to change this and somehow find out a way to save enough money to purchase a car for myself. I put in an application at the nearest grocery store, and within a week, they called and wanted me to come in for an interview. I was very excited but also nervous at the same time. I wanted the job so much because I desired to put my parents' discipline into action and prove to them they taught me well. A couple of days later, I received another phone call telling me I got the job.

When I first started working, I realized everything my parents told me was true: Work is not easy; you have to work hard and be an example to others around you, and saving money is harder than it sounds. When I got my paycheck, I decided I was going to set aside 10 percent of it to put toward a car. This did not work very well because my paychecks were not very much money, and only saving that amount would not even cover my car insurance for the month. I knew another approach had to be taken.

My next plan was to save the entire paycheck and only buy the things I needed. I also decided I would treat myself twice a week to anything I wanted, just as a treat to pay off for my hard work. I quickly realized this method was effective in both saving and also keeping me happy and upbeat; I was going to stick to it.

Today, I am happy to say I have saved enough money to purchase my own vehicle. Although I have enough money to buy something now, I decided to wait until the end of this summer so I can have save more money in order to get a more valuable car.

In conclusion, without the help of my parents' discipline and the self-motivation I had, I would not have learned the amount of hard work and dedication it takes to save money and achieve my goals. This really did prove to me I can do anything I put my mind to.

Saving for college

Saving for college is a little different from saving for other items you want to purchase, and for a few different reasons:

- Your parents may already be saving money for you to go to college.

- You may not know which college you want to attend, and therefore, you don't know the full cost of attending.

- You might be able to get scholarships and grants that will lessen the total cost you must pay.

- You may not even be sure you want to attend college, which can make it difficult to get motivated to save

If you are undecided about whether you will attend college or not, there is certainly no harm in putting some money aside in case you eventually decide you do want to go. Pay attention to where you put your college savings. Some accounts are designed specifically for college savings, and if you decide not to go and to use the money for another venture, you may lose a lot of the money in the account. For example, some state-sponsored programs allow parents to pre-purchase college tuition when a child is young so that child can someday attend a state college with the tuition already covered. Depending on the state, however, the money put toward tuition might not be refundable if the child does not decide to someday go to a state school.

CASE STUDY: SCHOLARSHIPS FOR SCHOOL

Shawna — Future College Student

To think I didn't have to worry about finances when I went to college was naive of me. I grew up thinking my college was paid for. I had it all planned out: I was going to go to the University of Florida. I was also planning to receive financial aid along with social security and have money left over. Surprisingly, life threw some curves at me.

It first started with my mom being out of state for two months, which ended up being when the applications were due for college scholarships. With my mom gone, my dad and I didn't have enough money to use for the applications, so I accepted the fact I wasn't going to go to a big university. I started to look at Central Florida Community College when I became interested in a college that, unfortunately, was in Georgia. I knew we didn't have enough money to send me to an out-of state private college or even to pay the application fee, so I wrote them a letter. They sent me a priority application and fee waiver application. I sent in the application and was accepted right away.

As I started to fall in love with Shorter College, I realized my preparations for college were not what I had intended. I recently found out my social security stops after I graduate from high school. My parents and I dealt with the situation. In reality, we couldn't afford a private, out-of-state college, but my heart was already there. I notified Shorter about this problem, and they sent me information. I ended up getting an out-of state scholarship, and there was a scholarship coming up that I would qualify for if I scored at least a 24 on my ACT. That scholarship alone would pay for 100 percent tuition, room and board, and any other expenses I had. The only thing that was stopping me from taking my ACT was that we couldn't afford it, and my family didn't qualify for a waiver. Thankfully, my brother paid for it.

I've never been so stressed than while waiting for the results from my test. My heart broke when I received a 23 on the ACT. I again started looking back into CFCC. A couple of weeks later, my scholarship coordinator was hounding me about going to a FAFSA meeting, so I went thinking it would be a waste of time. I left the meeting encouraged and set on going to Shorter. I found out I can classify as an independent and receive a good amount of money from the government.

Since then, I have been praying and applying for as many scholarships as I can. With many people's help, I have come a long way. I'm now looking forward to moving to Georgia and have learned you should never give up, even when things look doubtful.

Find out if your parents have set any money aside for you to go to college, and if so, what kind of accounts they have established for you. Is the money sitting in a regular savings account, or is the money tucked away in an account specific to educational savings? How much money do they already have saved for you to attend college, and how much money do they anticipate having saved by the time you head off to college? If you are already in college, and receiving financial assistance from your parents, you should still ask these questions to find out if there is enough money available for you to continue with your degree without needing to find a way to pull together extra money.

What is the difference between a regular savings account and an account specifically for education? A regular savings account earns interest that can be taxed, and you can generally pull the money out and use it however you like. An account specifically designated for educational spending is different. Depending on the type of account, the interest earned on the account may be non-taxable, and you may be restricted in how you utilize the money. For example, you may be able to withdraw money to pay for tuition and to buy books, but you cannot use the money to pay for your road trip to an amusement park.

CASE STUDY: SAVING MONEY ON COLLEGE

Excerpt from "How to Go to College on a Shoe String: The Insider's Guide to Grants, Scholarships, Cheap Books, Fellowships and Other Financial Aid Secrets" By Ann Marie O'Phelan, M.F.A

You can place money in a regular savings account at a bank, but you probably are going to earn a low interest rate, and you will have to pay federal and state income taxes on what you do earn. A better place to stash your college fund is a Section 529 plan. These plans are administered by states, so the rules and regulations vary from state to state. The money that is placed into these plans is tax-deferred, but the bonus is that qualified disbursements are not taxed, either. This allows parents to get the most bang for the buck. Even if you do not think you can save very much, putting at least some money into such a plan will have a financial benefit.

Another way of paying for college ahead of time is through a Section 529 prepaid tuition plan. The major benefit of this plan is that it allows you or your parents to lock in in-state tuition at public schools at current prices. If you purchase half a year's tuition, it will always be worth half a year's tuition, even five, ten, or 15 years later. Of course, this plan will only be worthwhile if you actually do attend a public school in your state. But if that is what you want, it can be a great way to avoid steep tuition increases. Like the 529 savings plan, prepaid tuition is now counted as a parental asset, so you can still qualify for financial aid even if all of your tuition is already paid for.

If you have been saving for a few years now, you may have a Coverdell Educational Savings Account (ESA). These accounts, often called somewhat erroneously Education IRAs, were created under the Taxpayer Relief Act of 1997. Anyone — grandparents, friends, and cousins — can contribute up to a total of $2,000 per year to these accounts. These accounts are treated as an asset of the owner for financial aid purposes. In most cases, this will be the parent, but ownership will pass to you when you reach age 18, unless provisions were made for your parents to retain ownership. Unless that happened, the account will be come your asset and could reduce your aid eligibility. A disadvantage of the Coverdell accounts is that contributions are taxable, although withdrawals for higher education purposes are not.

If your parents have saved enough money for you to attend college without contributing any of your own money, that's great. You will probably still want to save some money for college yourself in a regular savings account, though, because there will undoubtedly be plenty of expenses that you may not want to ask your parents to cover. It is one thing to ask your parents to pay for your textbooks, but it is another thing to ask your parents to pay for the oversized stuffed college mascot doll you may want to buy to put in your dorm room.

You want to have the freedom to go get pizza when the mood strikes, or to head to a movie when you need a break from studying. Unless your parents give you full financial support — including money for unnecessary expenses — you will need to pay for these type of expenses yourself. Because these purchases fall into the category of "wants," they certainly should not be paid for using credit cards. If you already have a nice cushion of money that you set aside specifically for these expenses, you will be able to indulge in fun stuff. Keep in mind that this does not mean you should use your emergency fund for fun purchases; this is another savings account entirely.

Did You Know?

"Going to college will help you earn more later in life and is a good investment — probably the best investment you will ever make."

Ken Washer, DBA, CFA, CFP, associate professor of finance
Creighton University

If you discover your parents have not saved any money toward your college education, try not to despair. You can obtain financial aid and scholarships to help you pay for the cost of attending college. Make an appointment to speak to a financial aid representative at the college you want to attend or your high school college counselor, and start saving now — no matter how long you have before you anticipate starting college. It does not matter if you will start college in five years or in five weeks; any amount of money you save will be helpful.

A word about financial aid: Don't assume you won't qualify. Even if your parents make a lot of money, there may be programs available to you. Look for scholarships and grants to help you, but don't stop saving.

Student loans

Student loans make sense if:

- You haven't saved enough money to pay for college.
- You do not qualify for financial aid and cannot obtain enough scholarships to fully pay for school.

- You cannot work enough hours to pay for school and keep up with your studies at the same time.

Here is something to keep in mind: Not everyone gets student loans. You may assume that everyone who enrolls in college obtains student loans, but that simply isn't true. There are many people who never obtain a single student loan because they either pay for college out of pocket (from working, saving, or through financial aid or scholarship), or because they only attend classes when they can afford to pay for the tuition and books without borrowing money.

There are two categories of student loans available: federal loans (loans after by the government) and private loans. Federal student loans usually feature a low interest rate and are available to students who may not have a credit history yet. This is the type of loan most college students start out with because of the low interest rate, the general ease of getting the loans, and the special programs available that can delay payments until after graduation. There are two types of federal student loans: the Stafford loan (the main type of loan most students receive, which can either be subsidized — meaning the government pays the interest — or unsubsidized — meaning you pay the interest, or payments are deferred until after graduation) and the Perkins loan (awarded to student with exceptional financial need). You can find out more about federal student aid by visiting the government's student aid website at **www.fafsa.ed.gov**. Completing a FAFSA form is the first step to applying for federal student aid and can be done on the government's website. For help understanding federal student aid or filing out your FAFSA form, talk to your college counselor at your high school.

Private loans come from lenders and usually have higher interest rates. They may also only be available to students who have good credit scores or who do not have negative items on their credit reports. Students may decide to take out a private student loan because the student loan they received from the government was not enough to cover all of their educational expenses. Sallie Mae (**www.salliemae.com**) is one private organization offering student loans. Check with your bank to see if they offer any type of student loan for their customers.

You can apply for a student loan in your own name, or your parents can apply for a student loan for you. A type of parent loan is the PLUS loan, or the Parent Loan for Undergraduate Students, which is a federal loan and lets parents borrow money to cover educational expenses not already covered by the student's financial aid package.

If you're befuddled by the various options you have regarding financial aid, visit the FinAid website (**www.finaid.org**) for a thorough discussion of all the various types of aid, including federal aid, private aid, savings, military aid, and scholarships.

Find Out More

Sallie Mae (**www.salliemae.com**) and FinAid (**www.finaid.org**) are great resources for information on student loans for undergraduate and graduate college students.

Getting student loans to pay for college is actually quite easy, but for some people, the prominence of loans can be a real problem. When money is so easy to obtain, some students may not work as hard to earn money from working, or may not be as careful with their money as they should be since they know they can get money from student loans.

Don't fall into this trap. Even though student loans can be useful, and may be considered a good idea if your college education eventually pays off in the form of a high-paying career, you don't *have* to get student loans. Consider working while attending college and aggressively pursuing scholarships and grants. Imagine what it would be like to graduate from college with thousands of dollars of debt on your shoulders. If you can avoid this outcome by working extra hours or carefully budgeting your spending, why wouldn't you?

Remember that student loans have to be paid back eventually. They are not free money and should not be viewed as something that naturally comes with being a student.

CASE STUDY: LEARNING INDEPENDENCE
Ashley – High School Student

The experiences I have faced while saving for a car have made me realize there is a difference between the things that you want and the things that you need. It has also taught me how to be independent. With the little amount of free time I have during the weekends and weekdays (I am an officer in a large service club, and a varsity cheerleader), I had to apply to jobs that would hire 16-year-olds and work around my hours. I filled out an application at a grocery store, and they hired me for two days a week because of my active and busy schedule.

Working only 20 hours in two weeks is not enough money to pay for a new car, insurance, gas, and other expenses. It became even more difficult when I wanted to go shopping, and I had to remember to buy only the things I needed, instead of the things I wanted. Because my paycheck is only $50 per week, I had a limited selection of cars to choose from. So, I couldn't really be picky, and I had to choose something that had four wheels, runs fine, and will get me to the places that I needed to go. These experiences have helped me learn the value of hard work and grow into the person I am today.

Saving for a rainy day

Emergency funds were discussed in Chapter 3, so you are already familiar with the concept of saving money with no specific purchase in mind. An emergency fund is not only set aside as a way to cover emergencies like medical problems or damage to your house or car from natural disasters. An emergency can be something as simple as fixing a flat tire or covering your necessary living expenses while searching for a new job. In other words, you don't have to be in huge financial peril in order to utilize your emergency fund. It is a smart move to put money away in an emergency fund; you never know when you may need extra money.

Saving money with no particular goal in mind can be tough. If you aren't saving for a tangible expense like a car or concert tickets, you might lose motivation and stop saving your extra money. In order to stay motivated, set a goal. Don't just tell yourself, "I'll save extra money when I can." Instead, tell yourself, "I will put away 3-6 months worth of expenses in an emergency fund." Here's how to actually make this goal happen:

1. Determine how much money you would need to cover all your expenses for approximately five months. Keep in

mind that this amount will change as you get older. If you live with your parents right now and don't have many expenses, the amount of money you need in order to cover five months' worth of expenses will be a lot different than when you eventually move out of your parents' house. For this reason, when your situation changes you should review how much money you have sitting in your emergency fund and determine how much additional money you need. Once you reach a point where you can comfortably sustain yourself for a few months with the money in your account, any extra money may have the potential to earn more interest in a different type of account, like an investment account or some other form of savings.

2. Take a look at your monthly expenses and write down the approximate amount of money you need to cover all your bills and necessary purchases. If you maintain a spending log, this will be a simple task, but if you don't keep track of your spending, it may take you a little longer to accomplish this. Once you have this amount figured out, multiply the total amount of your monthly expenses by the number of months you want to cover in your emergency fund. Preferably, you want to cover six months of expenses in your emergency fund, but three months' worth of expenses is still an incredible amount of money to have stashed away — and definitely more than most adults have in their savings account. The formula for determining how much money you should have in your emergency fund looks like this:

> **Monthly Expenses X 6 (Months)** = Amount of money you should have in your emergency fund

Don't get overwhelmed when you see the final amount. It may seem like a huge chunk of money, and this can make you anxious as you try to figure out how to save that much. Don't stress out. How do you get so much money together? The answer is simple: one dollar at a time.

There is no huge rush in gathering the funds for your emergency fund. Obviously, the quicker the better, but realize that this isn't something that will happen overnight. Building an adequate emergency fund is an ongoing process, and something many people still work on well into adulthood. A 19-year-old with half an emergency fund is better prepared for a financial problem than a 40-year-old with no money in savings whatsoever. It isn't the amount of money you have in your emergency fund that is so important; it is the amount of money related to what your expenses actually are.

Look at the final amount of money you want to have, then determine how much money you need to save every month to make it happen within the timeframe you are aiming for. How do you decide on a timeframe? This depends on how much money you can afford to put toward your emergency fund on a regular basis.

Suppose you estimate you should have approximately $4,800 in your emergency fund because your expenses are roughly $800 each month and you want to have six months' worth of expenses sitting in the bank. If you set the goal of having the emergency fund fully funded within a year's time, you will need to put $400 into the account each month. This probably is not a realistic scenario unless you have ample money left over every month from your expenses. If you can handle saving $400 a month, that's great! Otherwise, adjust your goal accordingly. Stretch out the timeframe for achieving your goal or adjust the total amount of money you want to put into your emergency fund. For example, if you decide to work toward a three-month emergency fund instead of six, you can put less money into your account each month and still reach your goal. Once you reach the goal of saving three months worth of expenses, move on to six months and then, eventually, a year.

Goal-setting is a very important aspect of managing your personal finances. Think about how you feel when you study a lot for a huge test and then ace it with flying colors. You know you earned the impressive grade through your hard work and sacrifice. Doesn't that feel great? The same principal can be applied to personal finances. Not only does it feel great to know you have met the financial goals you set for yourself, but you're likely to manage your finances more effectively when you realize how much hard work you've put into saving.

Saving for an emergency can seem a little abstract. You might not feel as motivated about plunking your money into a savings account as you would when saving money for something such as a car or concert tickets. But remember: Saving for an emergency before something actually happens will allow you to live comfortably and happily when the need does arise.

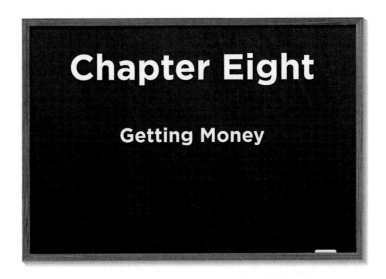

Chapter Eight

Getting Money

You've been reading about money for a while now. What if you don't have any, or don't have any means for making it? Rest assured that as you get older, you will have more opportunities to make money, but if you have never really earned an income before, it can all seem a little confusing. It really isn't a difficult concept: Find the best job you can while earning the most money possible. The goal is to earn an income while also doing something you enjoy or that stimulates you. Think about how frustrating it would be to earn a lot of money but have a job you hate going to each day, or to have a job you love but not have enough money to buy the things you need. It's important to find a balance. You may already have an income. Maybe you are already employed, or your parents give you a steady income in the form of an allowance. Whatever your situation, there is usually room for improvement. Perhaps you need to make more money, or you aren't very happy with your place of employment. Read on for tips on how to get the job you want, making the money you need.

CASE STUDY: YOUR FIRST JOB

Stephanee — Former Student

My first job was at a grocery store. I started working right after the beginning of my junior year in high school. I started out working about 30 hours a week and had some fluctuations, but by end of junior year, I was working at least 36 hours a week, some weeks up to 48. Until I started driving myself (as in, my mom got tired of doing it and would let me), my mom would pick me up right after school at 2:45; I would change in the van; and she would drop me off at work to start at 3. If I was working eight hours, I would get off at midnight. I almost always worked until 9 p.m. If I started at 4 p.m., I would get off at 10 p.m.

So, a typical weekday for me, as a junior in high school, went like this:

> 7 a.m.: Start school day. I was taking an early-morning class to get my athletics credits.
> 7:45 a.m.: Work on homework. I also did homework throughout the school day.
> 2:45 p.m.: Get out of school.
> 3 p.m.: Start work at the grocery store.
> 7 p.m.: Eat dinner at work (frozen dinner, sandwich, etc.).
> 12 a.m.: Get off work, picked up by my mom.
> 12-1 a.m.: Do homework, and then go to bed.

I usually had one day off during the week, and sometimes I had two days off. I liked working at least two of the 3 p.m. to 12 a.m. shifts because that meant I got more school days off with still a lot of income.

Why did I work? I wasn't able to play any sports or participate in any school extracurricular activities, so I couldn't partake in athletic games, and I couldn't try out for the tennis team. I couldn't be in band because of the money issue. However, when I saw the job posting for Albertson's, I took a chance and asked my mom. She said yes, took me to the interview, and I was hired. I had money and could buy clothes, food, or anything else I wanted. I also had awesome health insurance that included orthodontics — which I wanted really badly; I was eligible for orthodontics after two years of employment.

Did my parents care about my long work hours? I think they figured it kept me out of trouble, and they didn't have to buy anything for me anymore. I hardly ever ate at home, either; I bought all my meals.

Because I was at work so much, I missed out on other things at school. I never took the PSAT or other college entrance tests. What good came of working? I gained independence, self-confidence, and the value of a dollar.

I learned how to save, how to overspend, and how to run out of cash quick. My parents had me start paying $100 per month in rent starting the month I turned 18, and by time I was 20, I had bought my own car, taken two trips, paid for a year of college with my own money, and paid for my own auto and health insurance. When I moved out, I was able to balance my budget, and within five years, bought my first house for $135,000, and was able to put $20,000 down.

I will not encourage my own children to work like I did. Summer jobs and working on a Saturday morning are all right, but to me, it is not all right to work during the school year. I want them to get straight-As, volunteer, join clubs, play sports — whatever they want — but be well-rounded and eligible for scholarships. I want them to enjoy their teenage years.

Getting an Allowance

Depending on what state you live in, you may have to wait until you are 15 or 16 before you can go out and get a regular job with an employer. If you are not yet at the age to get a job outside of the home, or if you just want to concentrate on your school work and not bother with a job right now, you still have options for earning an income. If you do not get an allowance, it may be time to approach your parents about giving you a regular weekly allowance that will allow you to budget your money, as well as practice saving and spending carefully. If you already get an allowance, but don't feel like you get enough money to cover all your expenses, it may be time ask for more money. The amount of money you receive for your allowance depends on how much money your parents are willing (or able) to give. Don't assume that it is time to get a bigger allowance just because you always run out of money before the next allowance comes. Use the tools you have already learned about budgeting and managing your money to make sure that you are actually spending and saving like you should.

Here are some tips for approaching your parents about giving you an allowance or increasing the amount of allowance they already give you:

- Ask to speak about this topic during a time when you both aren't in front of the television or otherwise engaged in something. This is a discussion you should have between you and your parents without any distractions, if possible.

- Come to the discussion prepared. Be ready to defend your need for an allowance and to stay calm if your parents initially react badly. Your parents may say something along the lines of, "Why would you need an allowance? We already give you everything you need." or "If you want money, go get a job." While there is no surefire way to guarantee your parents will agree to give you an allowance, you are more likely to be successful in your request if you come to the discussion with a written budget of your expenses than you would if you tell your parents you need more money "just because." Show your parents the expenses you would like to take over if they agreed to give you an allowance. Tell them you want to learn to be responsible for your own money.

- Stay calm. The last thing you want to do is turn this into an argument with your parents. Think about the image you want to portray. Do you want your parents to think of you as a responsible teenager who has thoroughly thought through the request, or would you rather seem like you are coming to them whining about how everyone has money except for you? Your presentation of the subject is key in getting the allowance you want. If you whine or bicker, your parents are likely to not take your proposition seriously.

- Be prepared to bargain. Your parents may have a few demands before they will agree to an allowance. Maybe they want you to start doing certain chores around the house, or perhaps they want you to achieve a certain grade point average before they will agree to give you money on a regular basis. You have to be willing to compromise. You'll also need to stick to your side of the bargain. If you say you'll wash your parent's car each weekend, and you don't, be prepared to have your allowance taken away. It's just like a job; if you don't show up to work, you don't get paid.

- Keep in mind that some parents just can't afford to give you what you want. The truth is, some parents do a pretty good job of hiding the fact they are having financial problems — especially when hiding the financial problems from their teens. So, if your parents are adamant about the fact that they cannot give you an allowance or increase the amount they already give you, you may just have to accept it for now and find another way to earn an income.

CASE STUDY: HOW TO PICK THE BEST JOB

Clayton — Career Adviser

When looking for your first job, you should consider two things. First, is this a job you want to make as your career? If you feel it is the right time in life to start your career, then you should ask yourself: Is this a job you can see yourself enjoying in 10, 20, or even 30 years down the road? You should pick a job that's right for you, and not just any job in order to have work. Secondly, consider searching for a job you can build your career on. Many people don't stick with their first job, but they use it as a major step in gaining experience in the workplace. They also can gain personal skills such as people skills, computer skills, listening skills, and countless others. Not only can a first job help you find out new qualities about yourself, but it can also help you develop strong working skills. As your qualities and work skills grow, you can use them as a major tool in today's workforce.

My next point touches on how to write your first résumé. When writing a résumé, you must remember that no experience is too big or small. Even such things as mowing lawns during the summer can be listed as job experience. Also, a résumé is not just a list of jobs you have had in the past; it should also should list service hours, extracurricular activities, awards, and many other things you have accomplished. Just remember:

Your résumé is not a list of what you haven't done; it's a list of what you have done.

My final point to discuss is the interview, which is a crucial step in the process of getting a job, because this is your one chance to show the interviewer why you would be an asset to his/her company. Even if you are applying to a fast food restaurant, the interview is important. You only have one change to make a first impression, and with this impression, you can be hired or rejected. It is important to remember this is a business meeting, so you should act and look professional. This includes such things as not wearing flip-flops or chewing gum. Watch your body language. Be careful to not look at your watch as if you have somewhere else more important to be. You can improve their first impression by looking at your interviewer in the eye to show them you care about this job, answering their questions honestly, and being yourself so they can see your great personality. When looking for a job, you should consider finding a career that will fit your interests, help you to develop good working skills, and add to your résumé. By following these guidelines, you could be on your way to the career you have always wanted instead of settling for anything that passes your way.

Getting a Job

There comes a time when an allowance just isn't going to cut it anymore. Whether it's because you're heading off to college, or you want to buy your first car, getting your first job can be exciting.

The age when you can start working varies from state to state. In some instances, you can start working at a regular job around age 14 or 15, but you may need to get a consent form signed by your parents. Visit the U.S. Department of Labor's website **www. dol.gov/dol/topic/youthlabor/** to find more information on what hours and specific jobs you can work as a teen and how to prevent workplace injuries. You may also be limited in how many hours you can work and what type of work you will be allowed to do.

You don't have to settle for a job you hate. Many teens fall into the trap of thinking they have to start at the very bottom with a miserable position and work their way up, but this is not always the case. Of course, there may be some instances where the only job you qualify for is doing something relatively miserable, but if you are creative in your job search, you may be able to start out with a job you really enjoy.

What do you like to do? Don't just apply for every job you can think of. Think about what interests you and then pursue a job in that field. Do you like dealing directly with people? Try a service job like a restaurant where you will be in constant contact with people. Do you adore fashion? Find a job at a retail store. Do you love horses? Apply to work at a stable. Are you artistic? Spend some time volunteering at an art museum, then apply for a part-time job there. Your options are wide open because you have not yet established yourself within a certain field. As long as you have the confidence to apply for the job you really want, there is a chance you can wind up working somewhere great.

Also, consider looking for a job that will help your résumé or college application in the future, like answering phones or running errands for a law firm. These types of jobs offer experience that may be pertinent to a future career, or to a degree you wish to seek while in college. Many young people don't even try to get these types of jobs and instead settle for cashier job because they thing they don't have a shot — but they do.

Why is it so important to find a job you will actually enjoy? You will be more likely to look forward to going to work, and you will probably excel much more than if you have a job you didn't like.

Working does not have to be miserable, especially if you actually enjoy what you do.

When looking for a job, it is important to impress your potential employer. In some cases, if you can impress a potential employer enough, the company may not even care about your work experience or your level of education. Play up your extracurricular activities in school — you never know when your interviewer will say, "That's what I did in high school!" Are you a reporter for your high school's newspaper? Are you in drama or band? If you're in college, are you a member or a sorority or fraternity? You might be surprised by how much people associate themselves with these activities. If you come across an employer who was a member of your sorority, you might have just found your hook-up for the job.

Today, the U.S. unemployment rate is more than 10 percent. This means that 10 percent of people who want to work are not actually working. This is an incredibly large number. What does this mean for you? You will have more competition for jobs — even jobs that are traditionally held by teens or young adults, such as cashiers, cart pushers, or secretaries. Due to the current economy, many people have been laid off from their jobs and are now looking for new jobs. Unfortunately, there are far more workers than there are new job positions available. Older workers who typically have higher-ranking positions are willing to take on lower-paying jobs, and this leaves teens and young adults competing for jobs with people who may have a more impressive résumé. How do you combat this?

- **Be confident**. Confidence is an amazing attribute that can influence people into thinking you have reason to be confident. For example, if you apply for a job with a florist, and the florist asks you if you have any experience with arranging flowers, don't say "No, not really." Instead, reply with something along the lines of, "I enjoy arranging flowers for my family all the time. My family looks forward to my Thanksgiving centerpieces every year!" Don't lie, but don't downplay your abilities.

- **Be professional**. Don't stroll into a store wearing sweats and chewing gum and ask to speak to a manager because you want to apply for a job. Dress as you would if you were starting your first day of work. Until you find a job, your job is searching for one. Write up a résumé highlighting your experiences and always dress cleanly and modestly when applying for a job or attending an interview.

- **Be prepared**. Practice interview skills like making direct eye contact, giving firm handshakes, and answering questions about yourself without tripping over your words. Ask your parents or your friends to conduct practice interviews with you where they ask you questions and you answer them as confidently as possible.

Once you do get a job, sign up for direct deposit if your employer offers it. This allows your employer to deposit your pay into your bank account instead of giving you a paper check you have to deposit in the bank yourself. Not only is it convenient, but direct deposit usually allows you to have quicker access to your money. Signing up for direct deposit is usually a simple process, so ask your boss about getting your pay directly inserted into your bank account.

Resources for Finding a Job

Clueless as to how to go about finding the perfect job for you? Try these helpful resources:

- **Internet**: The Internet is the top resource for finding a job in today's economy. websites such as Beyond.com (**www.beyond.com**), CareerBuilder (**www.careerbuilder.com**), Hound (**www.hound.com**), and Indeed (**www.indeed.com**) are some of the most popular job-search websites.

- **Your local newspaper**: Almost all local newspapers have a classified section, and within that section, you will find job postings. This also might be a resource for posting notices about services you offer if you decide to create your own job instead, as detailed in the next section of this book.

- **Friends and family**: Sometimes, when in the midst of job searching, it's all about who you know. Does your mom know someone who works for a law firm? Ask her to find out if they need an errand runner. Is your cousin a nurse in a doctor's office? Ask her if they need someone to answer phones. Does your roommate work as a server in a restaurant? Ask him if they're hiring.

Create Your Own Job

Maybe there are no suitable jobs available where you live, or maybe the thought of working for someone else doing to same thing over and over again does not appeal to you. If the idea of going in to the same place every day and doing the same thing repeatedly for a small, hourly wage really turns your stomach, but you are motivated to start working, you may want to consider running your own business.

It isn't as complicated as it sounds. Creating your own business does not have to involve running an office or hiring a secretary. By operating your own business, you can provide services directly to one or more clients. For example, if you mow lawns for several houses in your neighborhood for money, then essentially you have your own mowing business. If you babysit for a few different families on a regular basis, you have a babysitting business. By doing this, you have found something you don't mind doing and have turned it into a profitable activity. The same can be said for someone who makes bracelets at home and sells them at fairs, or someone hired by companies to design websites.

There are advantages and disadvantages to having your own business. You get to decide when you want to work and you get to set your own prices. On the other hand, when you run your own business, you are the person in charge, and therefore, you are the only person who can take the blame when something goes wrong. For example, suppose you mow lawns in your neighborhood for profit, and one day you accidentally knock over an expensive bird bath with the mower. The bird bath shatters, and the homeowner wants you to pay for the damage. If you worked for

someone else, it is likely the company you worked for would pick up the cost of the damage. When you work for yourself, however, you would be the only person responsible, and would have to cover the cost of replacing the bird bath.

Working for yourself requires self-motivation. Suppose you are really good at calligraphy and create your own business addressing wedding invitations. A client pays you to address 100 invitations and wants them to be done in a week. If you wait until the last minute to start working on the project, it is likely you won't get it done in time, or you might deliver sloppy work to your client. Neither scenario is good for your business. If your work isn't good, the word will get around, and no one else will want to hire you.

If you are interested in working for yourself, try to think about things you like to do and how you can turn these activities into profitable ventures. If you love playing with kids, try babysitting. If you love dogs, start a dog-walking business. If you love spending time outside, offer to landscape your neighbors' yards. There is no limit to the things people will pay you to do, especially if you live in a neighborhood where almost everyone works outside of the home and have little time to take care of things like walking their dogs or grooming their lawns.

Here is a list of some ideas you can explore when deciding to open your own business:

- Babysitter
- Dog walker
- Craft/art creator
- Lawn mower
- Car washer
- House cleaner
- Errand runner
- Baker
- Writer
- Designer
- House sitter
- Tutor

You certainly aren't limited by this list. If you can think of something you love to do, and you know there are people willing to pay for it, go for it!

How do you know how much to charge for your services? Check out other local companies that offer the same service and see how much they charge. Make a couple of phone calls to these companies, or visit their websites to find out their prices. You should also charge based on your experience. If you're relatively new at your service, consider charging less until you gain more experience. Then, once you have established your business, people will pay you more because they know they can count on your expertise. Another idea is to offer customers service plan: Allow people in the neighborhood to choose from different packages, and keep tabs on everyone with a chart and an e-mail account.

CASE STUDY: OWNING YOUR OWN COMPANY

Peter — Entrepreneur and
High School Student

At the age of 13, I created my own company creating online Adobe® Flash entertainment. Flash allows designers to add animation and interactivity to websites or other software. Beforehand, I had no knowledge whatsoever as to how to manage a company, and I knew little about handling money or using it to reinvest in a business. While I didn't profit much from my company at first, I was soon required to communicate with sponsors and Web designers in order to create Flash games and to create a website that would later be profitable. The creation of my company and website serves as an example of how any teenager can use his or her skills to earn and save money for the future. With additional education and help from my parents, I was even able to invest in plans that would pay for college and retirement.

After familiarizing myself with Flash software in middle school, I began to submit my Flash games and animations to a free online portfolio. It was then that I decided I could create my own website and profit from my flash content. I was soon contacted by AddictingGames (**www.addictinggames.com**), a subsidiary of MTV, which was interested in my games, and I began to generate sales from T-shirts and by licensing my Flash games. The majority of my earnings were put in savings, and the remainder was used to hire other freelance professionals, through sites such as Elance (**www.elance.com**), to assist me in redesigning my website and the creation of my games.

My company, E19 Industries LLC, was created in 2006. It was later dubbed "Lawlolawl Studios." Most of my income at this point was generated by Google AdSense. About a year later, I was contacted by a representative of AddictingGames, who was interested in sponsoring my Flash game "!GNITION." The game was uploaded to their site, and my website traffic increased significantly. I became aware that Lawlolawl had over 30,000 individual users on it in a single day when the server crashed, so I decided to create a way to profit from the traffic on my site. To do so, I hired a specialist that worked with me to monetize my website.

Because I had plenty of visitors, I set up a simple store that enabled them to buy my T-shirts straight from my site. With the money coming in from my store, I was able to concentrate on freelance Web and game design, which included the creation of Flash website interfaces and games. Upon the release of new Flash content, I would send a newsletter to a list of 3,000 or so clients. In this way, I could continue to have traffic on my site, as well as ensure that my website's fans would purchase new products. I am currently working on a report describing how to profit from Flash games, and upon its completion, I can send an e-mail to my subscribers, offering them the product for an exclusive price.

As a child, I was taught to divide the money I received from gifts into two boxes: One, titled "temporary," held the money I could spend whenever I desired, and another, known as the "permanent" box, contained money I would save for college. Still following a similar process, the majority of the money I make from my website goes immediately into savings. After my bills are paid, I may use some money to purchase new Flash software or perhaps to hire an audio professional to create music for my game. Otherwise, the majority of my earned income is set aside for later in my life. After all, although it was a great experience to create my own company and website, my true intentions in doing so are to save money for the future. With assistance from my parents, the permanent money that Lawlolawl Studios generates goes into my own Roth IRA account. In addition, my parents have invested in a 529 plan for college and a whole-life insurance plan, which I will own when I become an adult.

> In the future, I plan on developing more ways to monetize my website in order to earn enough money to help with college expenses. Doing so will most likely require an expansion in my company that will tap in to my temporary savings. Nonetheless, as long as I continue to leave my permanent savings untouched, I am well-prepared for any possible financial issues. My parents have always stressed the importance of setting aside money for when you need it most. They must be right, because I have followed this principle and have come far.
>
> Lastly, I was taught it is important to share with others who are less fortunate. Currently, I donate 10 percent of the funds generated by E19 Industries to the Costa Rican Conservation Foundation (**www.fccmonteverde.org**), a non-profit organization whose primary goal is to protect Costa Rican wildlife through reforestation and educate others on the importance of protecting the environment. I am also working on redesigning their website, free of charge. I have the tools needed to make a difference at my disposal, and I plan to continue to use them.

Get rich quick?

When you are looking for a job or you are trying to think of ways to make money by working for yourself, be careful to avoid falling into the trap of thinking there are ways you can get rich quick without working hard. If you do a quick Internet search for a job you can do from home, for example, you will find plenty of "opportunities" that really aren't opportunities at all. These are nothing more than scams designed to lure people who are looking for work but who don't realize that people are out to take advantage of them. You aren't going to get rich stuffing envelopes or assembling products at home, which are just a few at-home jobs you will find on the Internet. You will probably not make a substantial amount of money by selling overpriced makeup or cleaning products to your family and friends; you cannot earn a living as an entry-level mystery shopper. Any company or individual that wants you to send money in order to learn how to make money is more than likely trying to scam you.

You should also avoid complicated financial schemes that are supposed to help people get rich quick. While it is true that people can make a lot of money doing things like buying and selling foreign currency, this is something that should be left to people who have studied the process and who have the money to spare. If you come across an ad or e-mail that says something along the lines of "Learn Money-Making Secrets!" or anything similar, don't believe the claims. If there were truly secrets to getting rich quick, don't you think the secret would have gotten out by now?

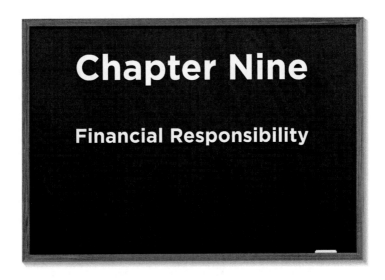

Chapter Nine

Financial Responsibility

Your degree of financial responsibility changes depending on how old you are. For example, suppose you are 14 years old and you accidentally break a car window while throwing a baseball around outside. Ultimately, it is up to your parents to cover the cost of replacing the window because you have not yet reached the age of financial responsibility as an adult. Now, suppose that the same scenario occurs, but this time you are a college student who is 21 years old. In this case, it isn't your parents who are going to be responsible to pay for the damage to the window — it's you.

Before you are 18, or in instances such as when a minor is emancipated, you will not be able to get credit on your own. This is because minors cannot legally enter into contracts without parental consent, and credit agreements are legal documents. In order to get a car loan or a credit card or even sign a contract for cell phone service, your parents must agree to the contract and sign alongside with you. If you default on paying your credit card bill, it becomes your parents' responsibility to pay. If your parents are like most parents, they probably will not be too happy about making your payments when you originally promised to cover the payments on your own. With your parents as cosigners, however, they don't really have a choice.

Cosigners and Joint Accounts

When your parents cosign with you, this means they assume financial responsibility if you don't pay. This does not mean the account ultimately belongs to your parents and they just let you use it. Instead, it is an account in your name, but in essence, your parents have vouched for you. The account appears on both credit reports: Yours and your parents.

The Credit Card Accountability, Responsibility, and Disclosure Act of 2009 mandates you can only get approved for a credit card in your name under the age of 21 if you have a cosigner or if you can prove you have the income necessary to pay your debts. How do creditors determine whether you have the ability to pay debts? They look at what is called the debt-to-income (DTI) ratio, which is the amount of money you are obligated to pay in debt payments compared to the amount of money you earn. If you don't have enough money coming in each month, and are under the age of 21, you will only be approved for credit if you get a cosigner.

If you are a minor under the age of 18, you can't enter into a financial contract on your own because minors aren't allowed to enter into legal obligations alone. With all of these restrictions in place to keep teens and college students from obtaining credit on their own, sometimes cosigning is the only option.

A cosigner usually does not have access to the account. For example, suppose you open a credit card account with your parents as cosigners. Even though they are financially obligated to pay the account balance, and the account will show up on their credit report and yours, they aren't allowed access to the card to make purchases. In other words, if you don't pay your bill, they will legally be responsible for paying it, but they don't actually get to spend the money on the card. It can be an odd position for your parents, so you should not be surprised if they are reluctant to cosign for you.

Another option is to open a joint account with your parents. This is different than cosigning because this account will belong to both you and your parents. You will all have equal access to the available credit, and each of you will be responsible for the payments. With this type of credit card account, everyone on the account can use the credit card to make purchases. If both of your parents are joint owners on the account, all three of you will get credit cards issued to you from the same account, and the monthly bill will have all three of your names on it. This is a common arrangement for parents to enter into with their teens and college students because it allows parents to keep a close eye on the spending on the account while also allowing the teen the ability to learn how to use a credit card.

Here is the most important thing to remember when it comes to having an account with your parents: It isn't only your finances on the line if you don't pay in a timely manner. Your parents have likely spent years building a good credit score. If you miss a few payments on your joint account, it will drag not only your credit score down, but theirs as well. You can see why they might be nervous about opening an account with someone who is totally new to the credit game.

If your parents are willing to cosign or open a joint account with you, be glad they trust you. If they are reluctant about opening accounts with you, or you have not yet asked them to do so yet, you may want to have a conversation about the following pros of a joint account when you are first starting out:

- A joint account can be closely monitored by the parents to make sure the teen is not spending recklessly.

- Teens who get practice managing credit early on may be better prepared to manage their credit when it is in their own name.

- A teen entering adulthood with an existing credit history may be in a better position to obtain low interest credit cards and loans than a person with no such credit history.

Many people start out their credit-driven lives by making mistakes that can haunt them for years afterward in the form of a bad credit rating or charged-off accounts. If you can begin with accounts your parents help you monitor, you may be better prepared when the time comes to start managing your credit all by yourself.

Parental access

Keep this in mind when you have an account with your parents: They can see everything you buy. Whenever you make a purchase with a credit card, your creditor makes a note of the purchase and lists it on your account activity log. This information is included on the monthly statement you receive from the credit card company and can usually be accessed easily by accessing your account on the credit card company's website.

Why is this so important to know? While you should periodically review the information on your credit card activity log to ensure there are no errors on the report, you should also be aware that this means that your parents can peek at what you have been buying with your credit card. Suppose your parents open a credit card account with you right before you head off to college, urging you to only use the card for emergency purchases. You then use the card to order pizza one night, but tell your parents the $20 charge was to pay a lab fee. All your parents have to do is look at the purchase activity on your statement, and it will become obvious the $20 didn't go toward a lab fee.

Your parents can also be listed as co-owners on your bank account. This is probably the case if the account was opened before your 18th birthday. If this is the case, your parents have full access to examine how much money you deposit and withdraw, as well as where you use your debit card, if you have one linked to the account.

Remember: Parents with access to your bank account also have the ability to withdraw funds. This may not be an issue for you, but teens and college students who have parents who are irresponsible with money should be aware there is always the possibility that their parents can wipe out the balance in their accounts. On the other hand, if you have parents who are responsible with their money and who can help guide you in managing your finances, it can actually be a very good thing for your parents to have access to your accounts.

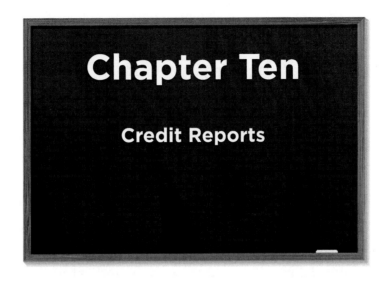

Chapter Ten

Credit Reports

Credit reports are histories of how you manage credit. If you have never had a credit card or loan, your credit report likely does not list anything except your current address and notes about credit applications you may have already filled out.

Why should you care about what is on your credit report? There are a few very good reasons:

- The information on your credit report dictates what credit you are eligible for.

- Potential employers may review a credit report before offering you a job.

- Potential landlords may also review your credit report before allowing you to rent an apartment or a house.

It's not just about getting credit. Your credit report and credit score paint a picture about how you manage your personal finances. If your credit report is full of negative items such as late payments or maxed-out credit limits, you may miss out on things beyond credit, such as getting a job or renting the place where you want to live.

What's Listed?

Not everything regarding your financial standing is listed on your credit report. For example, you won't find information on your credit report listing the banks accounts you have or how much money you make at your job. Instead, you will find information about the credit accounts, such as credit cards, car loans, and any other types of loans you have and your payment history on those accounts. Specifically, information regarding the length of time the account has been open, minimum monthly payment amount, balance, total credit limit, and whether the account has ever been 30 days (or longer) past due. Accounts you once had, but have closed, may be listed on the report, too, depending on how long ago they were closed.

Your current address is also listed, along with any other addresses you previously had when applying for credit. In addition to all this, any time you apply for a credit card or loan, a credit inquiry is placed on the report. This means a note is put on your credit report showing that a specific company looked at your credit report in order to determine whether to offer you credit. This means that if you apply for a credit card and are turned down, the fact that you applied will still be listed on your credit report under the inquiries list.

A good credit report has a few credit accounts listed with no late payments reported at all. It isn't uncommon to have one or two late payments on your credit report, especially when you are fairly new to managing your own credit. Keep in mind, however, that every single late payment puts a blemish on your credit report, and your credit score will be lowered as a result. When you are struggling to establish credit and raise your score, every little negative item on your credit report can have a huge impact.

Credit Scores

You have undoubtedly heard the term "credit score" tossed around quite a bit. A credit score is a three-digit number that automatically tells lenders whether you are credit-worthy. In other words, the three-digit number sums up your chances of repaying a loan based on how you have managed your credit in the past. A credit score is based on the length of time you have had credit, how you manage the accounts you have, and what type of credit you have. You start out with no credit score, and the score changes according to what you do with your credit. It takes a while to have a good credit score, but trashing your credit score can happen pretty quickly if you don't make your payments on time.

Did You Know?

You can review your credit report once a year at no charge at www.annualcreditreport.com. .

A credit score ranges from 300-850. According to Experian, most people have credit scores somewhere around 600-750. Here is what the credit scale looks like:

Credit Score Range	Credit Status
800 – 850	Excellent Credit
700 - 799	Very Good Credit
600 – 699	Average Credit
500 – 599	Fair Credit
400 – 499	Poor Credit
300 – 399	Horrible Credit

Where is your credit score? If you don't have any open credit account yet, or you have just recently opened your first account, you likely do not have a score at all. When ranking your credit worthiness, you don't start at the bottom and work your way up. Instead, your credit score is generated once you have a credit history to analyze. So, if you have new credit account that you pay on time and don't max out, you will have a better credit score than someone who has had credit for years but never pays on time.

Remember: The plus side of responsibly managing your finances, making payments on time, and using credit cards wisely is a good credit score. A good credit score is key to future success in many areas of your life. A good credit score allows you the ability to achieve basic things such as getting a job and buying a house.

Identity theft

As someone who has not yet established a lot of credit, you are at high risk for identity theft. Although this may seem backward, (wouldn't people with a lot of credit cards be most at risk?) the truth is, you are an ideal victim. You have probably not yet established a credit history, so this makes it easy for an identity thief to open an account in your name and remain undiscovered until

you either check your credit report or you begin getting bills in the mail from a company you never opened an account with.

When you review your credit report, you are making sure everything listed on the report is accurate and no one is using your identity to obtain credit. When you think about how many times a day people open new accounts, use credit cards, and close accounts, it shouldn't come as shock that mistakes happen on credit reports because there is always a constant stream of information for credit reporting agencies to process. Errors can get fixed, but when the error is a result of identity theft, the process of removing false information from your credit report cleared is more difficult.

When your identity is stolen, lots of different problems can occur:

- The identity thief might open up new accounts in your name.
- The identity thief might use the accounts you already have.
- The identity thief might sell your information to other identity thieves.

Who steals identities?

According to the Federal Trade Commission, some people who experience identity theft had their information stolen by some they knew. Friends, family members, and coworkers have all been known to steal information in order to open credit accounts in someone else's name, but more often it is a stranger who steals identities by getting access to personal information What information do they need to steal in order to open an account? Although application information requirements vary, here is the type of information an identity thief looks for:

- Full legal name
- Social security number
- Date of birth
- Account numbers
- Address

Information containing this information should be carefully safeguarded. Bills and bank statements should not be thrown away in the trash. Instead, you should shred them to make sure no one gets their hands on your information. It may seem weird to you, but some identity thieves will resort to digging through your trash to get your personal information.

Don't leave your purse or wallet lying around where other people have access to it, and don't reveal your account numbers and other personal information to people who don't need to know it. For example, suppose you ride with a friend to get lunch, but stop at a drive-thru ATM first to get cash. Your friend is driving, so in order to make things easier, you give your ATM card to your friend and tell him or her your PIN. What you don't realize is that your friend memorizes your PIN and later steals your ATM card. With your PIN and ATM card in hand, your "friend" can easily wipe out your account.

- Don't talk to your bank over the phone with someone else listening nearby.
- Don't use public computers to access your accounts.
- Don't use an ATM or input your PIN for a purchase if someone is watching over your shoulder.

Identity thieves can be strangers, too. Never reveal personal information via e-mail, pop-up websites on the computer, or telephone to someone you don't know. Someone may call you and claim to be a representative from your bank or credit card company, but unless you know this person personally, you just can't be sure. It may actually be someone posing as a representative, trying to get your account information. Your best bet in this situation is to hang up and call your bank or credit card company directly. By doing this, you can ensure you aren't giving your personal account information to someone who is trying to steal your identity.

You need to use caution with websites you aren't familiar with, as well as with websites you visit regularly, but something doesn't look quite right. Look for the padlock icon on the screen that tells you the site is secure, and if your computer features site advisor or site protection software, use it. Remember: Anyone with some Web knowledge can create a website that resembles a specific merchant's site. If you input your personal account information into a site you aren't familiar with, you may be sending the information right into the hands of an identity thief.

Help! Someone stole my identity!

What do you do if you find out someone has stolen your identity? How much work you have to do to repair any damage that has been done will depend on the extent of the identity theft, but there are some things you should always do if you think your identity has been stolen:

- **File a police report.** This is an important step because some lenders will require a copy of the police report in order to remove information from your credit report.

- **Review your credit report.** You should also file a fraud alert on your credit report, which is a statement that lets potential creditors know that you are a victim of identity theft. It will also stop new lenders from approving credit applications until they can verify your identity. Place a fraud alert on your credit report by contacting the credit bureaus either online or over the phone.

- **Don't give up!** There may be a lot of work involved in getting your name cleared of false accounts and charges, but it will be worth it in the long run. Remember: You are not financially liable for accounts opened in your name fraudulently by someone else, but creditors will probably still pursue you until the matter is cleared up.

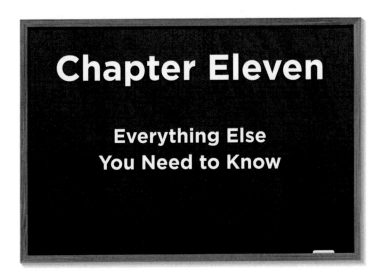

Chapter Eleven

Everything Else
You Need to Know

P at yourself on the back! You have already learned a bunch of financial information that will equip you for effectively managing your finances now and in the future. As you go through life, there will be plenty of new financial concepts to grasp, and you will need to constantly evaluate your money situation and find ways to stretch your dollars further. Managing your money is a constantly evolving process, but you are starting out in great shape because of your understanding of the basics (and more).

The next few topics are briefly discussed because you should know about them in order to manage your money as best as you can. Keep in mind, however, that these topics in particular can vary greatly depending on where you live, how much money you make, and what your living situation is.

Investing

Investing involves more than putting money into the stock market. An investment is a situation in which you put money into something you think will eventually make more money, therefore giving you even more money than you started out with. For example, a producer gives money to a theater company to put together a stage play with the hopes the ticket sales will be enough to make a profit for the producer. Another example of investing is buying a home, renovating it, and selling it at a higher price than you purchased it for.

Should you invest money right now? Here are some things to consider before investing in anything, now or in the future:

- **Can I spare this money?** There is always risk involved in an investment. Consider the producer who invests in the stage play. What if the play is a flop and no one buys tickets to see it? In this case, the producer loses his or her money. Always keep in mind that you should not empty out your savings account to invest in anything. Money spent to invest should be extra and should not compromise your ability to pay your bills or live with life's necessities.

- **Do I understand the investment?** Whether you want to buy stock in your favorite company, or you want to buy art you hope will be worth a lot of money someday, don't invest money in things you don't fully understand.

- **Am I ready for ups and downs?** You shouldn't expect your investment to always make money, especially if you invest in the stock market. Stocks go up and down — sometimes wildly — and if you are going to be a long-term investor, you will have to get used to your profits fluctuating.

Before investing, try out an online investment simulation program that allows you to practice investing before you actually spend the money. This can be the best introduction into the world of investing and will show you the possible outcome for any money you invest. Try **Investopedia.com** or **HowTheMarket-Works.com**'s simulator. For a site investment simulator designed specifically for young people, visit **www.weseed.com**.

Taxes

You get your first job and make $8 an hour. You work 15 hours in your first week and anticipate receiving a check for $120, but when your check arrives, it is for less than the expected amount. Why? When you work, whether you like it or not, a portion of your income goes toward taxes.

What are taxes? Taxes are charged by the government based on a percentage of your income. Not all states charge taxes, but you will be required to pay federal taxes. The government uses the money obtained from charging taxes to fund everything, such as fire departments, welfare programs, and the military.

The taxes you pay depend on what state you live in and whether your parents claim you as a financial dependent on their income tax forms or not. You will pay federal income tax and may also have state taxes to pay, depending on where you live. You will probably also have a portion deducted for social security and Medicare.

If you don't understand why money is being taken out of your paycheck, speak up! Talk to your boss or parents about the money being taken out of your paycheck and make sure you know where your money is going. Other possible deductions you might see on your paycheck, which are not necessarily related to taxes, include:

- Charitable contributions you signed up to contribute to.

- Retirement accounts, such as a 401(k). If the company you work for offers retirement accounts, signing up is usually a smart idea.

- Any amount of money you owe to the company for whatever reason, such as tuition reimbursement repayment or repaying a salary advance.

You will deal with taxes for as long as you live, so be prepared to routinely see money taken out of your paychecks to go toward taxes. For more information regarding taxes that is specifically designed for teens, check out **www.usa.gov**.

Insurance

Insurance is something designed to cover costs for an unexpected and substantial expense. You pay a set amount each month to the insurer, and the insurance company covers your costs if an event happens in which you need to utilize your insurance. Here are examples of common insurance policies:

- **Car insurance**: This covers the cost of replacing or repairing your car if you get into an accident and also pays for damage done to vehicles and property in an accident when you are the one at fault. Car insurance can also cover medical bills and other related expenses.

- **Health insurance**: This pays for the cost of medical care, either fully or partially, and is usually provided through employers or parents. You can buy health insurance on your own, but it is usually very expensive.

- **Life insurance**: This pays money upon your death to whomever you specify as your beneficiary. For example, if your mother is listed as your beneficiary on your life insurance policy of $50,000, she will receive that money if you die. Life insurance is not something you will likely need to be worried about at this point, but it is a good idea to be familiar with the term in case you hear others around you using it.

- **Homeowner/renter insurance**: This covers the cost of repairing the place you live and the property in the residence if a natural disaster or other covered instance occurs.

What insurance policies do you need right now? This is something you should talk to your parents or an insurance agent about, as it varies widely according to an individual's situation. However, a typical teen who lives with their parents may not need to purchase any additional insurance unless he or she purchases a car. If you are a college student residing in a dorm or off-campus housing, you will want to purchase renter's insurance to protect your property.

If you are not covered by your parents' health insurance coverage, look into obtaining health care coverage through the school you attend, the employer you work for, or through a state-sponsored program. Buying a full health insurance policy on your own may prove nearly impossible if you do not work full time.

If you want to learn more about insurance, check out the Junior Achievement website: **www.ja.org**.

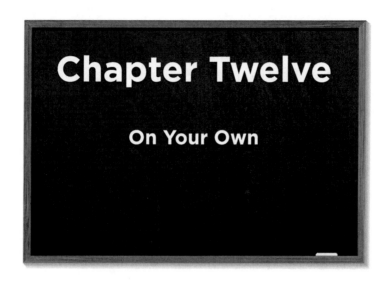

Chapter Twelve

On Your Own

Is it time to move out of your parents' house? Whether you are heading off to college or you are paying for your own place, it can be an extremely exciting time. This is not a decision you want to make lightly, however, because moving out of your parents' home before you are financially ready can set into motion a huge series of events that may put you in a bad financial position for years to come.

Making the Decision to Leave

How do you know it is time to move out of your parents' house? Sometimes it is an obvious choice, such as when you are heading to a college far away or your parents ask you to move out. For some people, though, moving out of your parents' home may just feel like the right thing to do. You may feel as though it is time for you to move on to the next chapter in your life, and moving out on your own is the logical step.

Talk to your parents about your intentions to move out. They may offer valuable advice to help you make your decision. Just be sure you aren't making this decision for the wrong reasons. It is one thing to move out because you want to live on your own when you have the financial means to do so, but it is another thing entirely to irrationally move about because your parents have made you mad. It is far better to be prepared — mentally and financially — for this huge next step.

You will know you are ready to move out of your parents' house when you have the ability to pay your own way. This means you have already written a budget based on how much money you will need to live on your own and your income is secure, whether from your parents or from a job. Keep in mind that living on your own is a lot different than living under your parents' roof. Take into consideration that there will be a lot of expenses you may never have had to worry about before, such as an electric bill, water bill, and other common costs associated with living on your own.

When you leave your parents' home, do it with some savings intact and a realistic budget already written. You will need to work extra hard to watch your spending to make sure you can cover all your expenses, especially in the beginning when you are learning how much money you actually need.

Remember: Unless your parents have asked you to leave the house, there is no reason why you shouldn't stay if you are attending a local college, or if you don't have enough money to support yourself right now. No, you don't want to live with your parents forever, but there is no magical birthday that automati-

cally signifies it is time to pack up and leave. This is something you should talk to your parents about. Discuss what your goal is with regards to moving out, and then come up with a financial plan to make it happen. After all, think about how much easier it will be to move out of your parents home after you have spent six months or a year working and saving up for your move.

What type of expenses will you have when you move out that you may not have right now while you live with your parents? Here is a brief list:

- Rent

- Utilities: Electricity, water, phone, and other necessary utilities

- Insurance: Health, car, renters, or homeowner's

- Food

- Repairs

Remember: Unless your parents agree to help cover the costs associated with living on your own, you will be solely responsible for any bills that need to be paid. You might be amazed at how quickly expenses add up when there is no one else to loan you money. Ask your parents to sit down with you and discuss the various expenses you may encounter that you might not be expecting.

The Current State of the Economy

Due to the recent decline in the economy, many teens are staying at home longer, and many college graduates are returning to their parents' homes because they are unable to find jobs. Before you venture off on your own, it's important to have a plan for how you will bring in income and know that you can cover all your expenses. Even college students who earned degrees in typically high-paying careers are being forced to return to their hometowns to live with their parents until a secure career becomes available.

If you think you're ready to carve your own path, talk with your parents first about their suggestions.

Budgeting Worksheet

Use the following budgeting worksheet to plan for expenses you might encounter once you move away from home.

Income		Expenses	
Your pay	$	**Rent**	$
Money from parents	$	**Utilities** (phone, gas, electric, and cable)	$
Tips	$	**Insurance** (home, auto, life, and health)	$
Other income	$	**Food** (eating out, ordering in, and school food plan)	$
	$	**School supplies** (pens, paper, and notebooks)	$
	$	**Clothing**	$

	$	**Auto** (gas and maintenance)	$
	$	**Cell phone**	$
	$	**Health** (medical, dental, and over-the-counter medications)	$
	$	**Entertainment** (movies, concerts, and music downloads)	$
	$	**Gifts** (holidays and birthdays)	$
	$	**Savings account** (try to save 10 percent of income)	$
	$	**Emergency fund/ incidentals**	$
	$	**Other expenses**	$
Total	*$*	*Totals*	*$*

Congratulations!

Y ou have every reason to be excited about having the tools you need to become financially responsible. As a teen or a college student, you are either on the brink of becoming an adult, or you've recently been thrust into adulthood. It will not always be easy, and you may encounter many financial setbacks along the way, but if you go into this new phase of your life with financial knowhow (and some savings to back you up), you may enjoy it much more than if you were struggling every day to make ends meet.

You *can* handle your finances on your own. Don't be nervous about asking for advice or help when you need it. Nearly everyone makes financial mistakes when they first start out, so don't take one mistake as proof that you can't manage your finances. Chalk it up to experience, learn from it, and move on. With all the knowledge you now have about managing your personal finances, you are ready to start managing your own money, whether you are still at home with your parents or out on your own.

Managing your personal finances is not complicated! Spend less money than you make, pay attention to what your money is doing, and stash some money away for the future. These are pretty simple ideas, even if they are associated with concepts like compound interest, annual fees, and deposit accounts. Many financial terms that sound complicated are simply fancy words for relatively easy-to-understand ideas. You don't need a degree in finance in order to manage your money effectively and prosper, especially if you start managing your money well at a young age.

Time is on your side right now. There are no adults around who will tell you, "I sure wish I hadn't put so much money into my savings account," or "I really wish I had more credit card debt to contend with right now." If you can start saving money for the future right now, and if you can avoid racking up unnecessary debt, you will put yourself into an excellent financial position many adults never find themselves in.

Struggling with finances is no fun. People who do not have enough money to pay their bills struggle considerably, and other aspects of their lives can suffer because of the stress they experience from their financial problems. With the tools you now have to effectively manage your money, you don't ever have to experience this.

"Pecunia, si uti scis, ancilla est; si nescis, domina — If you can use money, money is your slave; if you can't, money is your master"

-Ancient Proverb

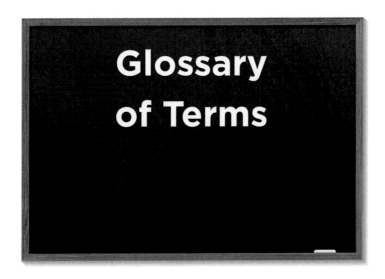

401(k) Plan: A savings account established by your employer that is specifically for retirement savings. The money you put into your 401(k) is not taxed until you use it. Some employers will "match" some of the money you put into the 401(k), which means for every dollar you contribute to your account, your employer will also contribute a dollar. This is a great benefit to look for when choosing whom to work for.

Account Agreement: The paperwork your financial institution gives you when you open an account. All the legal information about the account is listed in this agreement. By signing these forms, you are stating you understand how the account works.

Accounts Payable: The term used to refer to money a business owes to a person or company. For example, if you own a lawn mowing business and you owe money to the person who repaired your lawn mower, this payment falls under this account.

Accounts Receivable: Refers to money owed to a business, such as clients who owe you money for mowing their lawns.

Adjustable Rate Mortgage: A loan to buy a home that does not have a set interest rate. The interest rate can go up or down, depending on what the interest rate is based on. This type of mortgage is commonly referred to as an ARM loan.

Adjusted Balance: One of the methods used by creditors when determining the balance owed by borrowers. With this method, interest is charged on the principal balance after the credits and payments from the previous statement balance have been added to the account. Any new charges to the account will not begin to be charged interest until after the statement cycle ends.

Adverse Action: An action taken, usually not in your favor, as a result of negative aspects on your credit report. For example, if you are turned down for a car loan because of late credit card payments listed on your credit report, the denial of the car loan application is referred to as an adverse action.

Amortization: The amortization of a loan refers to a payment plan set up to allow the borrower to pay off the total amount owed, including interest charges, through regular payments. For example, car loans are commonly amortized for five years and mortgages are commonly amortized for 30 years.

Annual Percentage Rate (APR): The cost of the credit in percentage terms. The total APR cost includes interest and recurring fees on an annual basis. Although many people use the terms "interest rate" and APR interchangeably, these two figures can be different based on the type of credit product. In general, it is best to look for the lowest APR when getting a credit account to save money.

Appraisal: Determines what something is worth, usually real estate or personal property. An appraisal is contacted by a professional appraiser. Appraisals are usually used for real estate, cars, and other valuable items.

Asset: Something you own, including money you have in the bank or your car minus how much you owe currently to the bank.

Assumed Interest Rate (AIR): An insurance term referring to the interest rate an insurance company will pay out for insurance products that are designed to build wealth.

Automatic Deferral Default Percentage: The percent of your pay that an employer assumes you will contribute to an offered program. For example, when you enroll in your employer's 401(k) program, you will probably be enrolled using whatever the automatic deferral default percentage is unless you specify a different amount.

Automatic Rollover: When retirement savings are transferred into an individual retirement account (IRA) automatically.

Average Daily Balance: The average balance of your account, usually based on a month's worth of transactions. You will see the average daily balance listed on bank account statements as well as on credit card statements.

Balloon Loan: A loan that is amortized over a certain period of time, but come due in full earlier than the fully amortized terms. For example, a balloon mortgage might be amortized for 30 years, but at 10 years it must either be paid in full or refinanced. These types of loans are common for investors who want the advantage of a low monthly payment, but who also know they will not need the loan for the full term because they will sell the property.

Bankruptcy: Legal action filed by borrowers when they cannot handle their credit bills any longer. It is not an easy or simple process and can involve the total liquidation of debt and some assets (referred to as a Chapter 7 Bankruptcy) or a reorganization of debts where a new payment plan is created to give the borrower the chance to get a handle on debt (referred to as a Chapter 13 Bankruptcy). There are other types of bankruptcies offered for businesses. Bankruptcy severely damages the borrower's credit score and should be a last resort.

Beneficiary: The person who will inherit money or property when a person dies. This can apply to life insurance policies or financial accounts, or to property left in a will. For example, if your uncle states in his will that he wants everything he owns to go to you upon his death, you are his beneficiary.

Bonds: A form of saving where you provide money to the government or a corporation for a specified amount of time in return for interest paid by the organization issuing the bond. You will not have access to your money while it is in the bond, but this can be a good place to stash money you do not currently need.

Capital Growth Strategy: A plan you use to make the most out of the money you have invested or placed into savings products. Using a capital growth strategy, you will determine the best investment strategies to make the most profit.

Certificate of Deposit: A savings account that pays high interest at a set rate for a set period of time. You do not have access to the funds while they are in the CD, so this makes this form of saving a good idea for money you want to see grow within a certain amount of time.

Charge-off: This happens when a creditor decides to stop pursuing a borrower for a debt owed because the borrower is not likely to pay the debt. A charge-off usually happens after several months have passed without payment. A charge-off appears negatively on your credit report.

Closing Costs: The fees and taxes associated with the creation of a new loan. Closing costs are common with mortgage loans. While some closing costs are purely profit for the lender, some are necessary to pay real estate taxes or to file necessary documents associated with the loan.

Collection: Refers to the act of trying to get a borrower to pay a past due debt. Some lenders try to collect debt on their own while others use professional collection agencies for this task.

Compounding: When interest starts to get earned on interest. Suppose a savings account with a balance of $100 earns $0.25 in interest for the month. The next month, the interest earned will not be based on $100, but instead on $100.25. This is how money in savings accounts grows in addition to deposits made by the accountholder.

Consolidated Omnibus Budget Reconciliation Act (COBRA): Allows people who have health insurance through their employer to keep the health insurance even if they leave their jobs or are laid off. This is important because health insurance that is not provided through an employer plan can be incredibly expensive. COBRA health insurance may cost more than the health insurance cost while employed, but it will almost always be less expensive than buying health insurance without an employer-provided plan.

Consumer Credit File: The information assigned to you according to your social security number, listing everything related to your credit history, including current and past debts.

Consumer Finance: A term used in two different manners. It may refer to any type of credit product offered to borrowers, or to credit products specifically marketed toward people with bad credit.

Coverdell Education Savings Account (ESA): A type of college savings account that features tax advantages.

Credit Bureau: Equifax, Experian, and TransUnion are the three major credit bureaus, although there are other companies. These companies are not governmental agencies, but are instead businesses that record credit activity for individual consumers and report this information in the form of credit reports.

Credit Bureau Risk Score: A credit score based on information provided by the credit bureaus. The numerical score presented with a credit bureau risk score tells potential lenders whether a borrower is creditworthy.

Credit Opportunity Act (ECOA): Requires that all credit decisions from lenders be based solely on factors directly related to an applicant's ability or likelihood to repay debt. In other words, a lender can look at your payment history but not your gender when deciding whether or not to approve your credit application.

Credit Score: A three-digit score that is based on the information listed on your credit report. The higher your score, the more likely you will be approved for credit and be approved at a low interest rate.

Credit Union: A financial institution that is not-for-profit and uses the funds of the members to provide credit products to other members. Credit unions usually offer attractive products and generally have more personalized customer service than larger banks, but membership to a credit union is limited to eligible people.

Custodial Account: The name for an account opened and managed by someone on behalf of someone else. For example, if you put money into a mutual fund account, the allocation of your funds may be managed by the mutual fund company instead of by you.

Debit: Money taken from your account. For example, if you withdraw $20 from your checking account, this is considered a $20 debit from the account.

Debit Card: A card connected to your checking account with a financial institution. You can use the debit card to withdraw money from an ATM or by swiping the card at a store to pay for purchases. Unless otherwise specified, debit cards do not usually have credit cards accounts attached to them, but they may be have a Visa or MasterCard that which enables you to use the card at retail locations.

Debt Load: The amount of money a borrower owes in total. If you owe $4,000 for your car and $280 for your credit card, your total debt load is $4,280.

Debt-to-Income Ratio: A figure that reveals how much money you owe in debt in relation to how much money you receive from income. The lower your debt-to-income ratio, the better.

Defined-Benefit Plan: A retirement plan offered by employers that is based on factors such as how long the employee has worked for the company and how much money the employee makes.

Defined-Contribution Plan: A retirement plan through an employer where the employer contributes funds to the retirement fund on behalf of the employee.

Deflation: The opposite of inflation. This happens when the prices for goods and services declines.

Demand Loan: A loan that allows the lender to demand full payment of the loan regardless of the amortization.

Direct Deposit: Money that is deposited automatically into your bank account at a financial institution instead of being given to you in the form of a paper check.

Direct Rollover: When the balance from a retirement account is rolled into a different retirement account. A direct rollover avoids taxes and does not include the having access to the funds during the rollover.

Diversification: An investment strategy that involves dispersing money for savings or investments among different accounts or investment options. This is common with people who invest in the stock market because investors often do not want to lose all their money if the one company they invest in suddenly drops sharply in stock price.

Dividends: Money you will receive from a company if you invest in their stocks or mutual funds, and the company you invest in makes a profit.

Down Payment: The amount of money you pay toward a debt before the loan. For example, if you buy a car that costs $10,000 with a down payment of $1,000, the remaining $9,000 will be financed through a car loan. Having a large down payment can increase your odds of getting approved for a car loan or mortgage.

Early Withdrawal: Happens when you take money out of an account before the agreed-upon terms. For example, if you withdraw funds from a retirement account before you are of retirement age, this can be considered early withdrawal and will usually result in penalties.

Earned Income: The amount of money you make from an employer.

Employee Contribution Plan: A retirement account that is provided through an employer. Money deposited into the retirement account is withdrawn directly from your pay before you have access to the funds.

Endorse: The act of signing the back of a check in order to deposit or cash it.

Equity: The amount of money something is worth minus the amount that is owed on it. For example, a house worth $200,000 with a $150,000 mortgage balance has $50,000 worth of equity.

Escrow: Established to hold funds while a contract is being negotiated. Escrow is common with home purchases but is becoming more prevalent with online purchases. For example, a person purchasing a car online might put the money for the purchase into an escrow account until the car passes an inspection by the buyer.

Fair Credit Reporting Act (FCRA): States that consumers have the right to have accurate information listed on their credit reports and have a right to know what is listed within their credit reports.

Fair Debt Collection Practices Act (FDCPA): A federal law prohibiting abusive and unfair debt collection practices. This Act prohibits debt collection agents from using unreasonable or abusive actions in an attempt to collect debts from borrowers. The Act specifies how collectors can go about attempting to collect past-due debts.

FAFSA: An application that must be filled out by any college student looking to receive financial aid for school expenses.

FICO® Scores: This is the credit score assigned to every consumer by the Fair Isaac Corporation. How long a person has credit, as well as how they pay and maintain that credit, are factored into the scoring. The higher your FICO score, the better.

Fixed Rate: An interest rate that does not change. For example, if you receive a car loan at 6 percent interest, the rate of interest will always be 6 percent for the entire life of the loan.

Foreclosure: When a borrower stops making timely payments for a loan that has collateral, such as with a home loan, the lender can foreclose on the collateral. For example, if a homeowner stops making payments on a mortgage, the lender can foreclose on the home and take possession of the home.

Home Equity Line of Credit (HELOC): An account with a revolving line of credit, based on the equity within a home. The borrower's home is offered to the bank as collateral. These usually feature low interest rates and may have tax advantages.

Individual Retirement Account (IRA): A retirement account. Money you put into this account may be tax-deductible, although it varies according to the type of IRA you open. There are annual limitations regarding how much money you can put into an IRA, and money cannot be accessed without penalty until retirement age, except in certain circumstances.

Inheritance Tax: Tax paid on money you receive as a beneficiary when someone dies. Not all states have inheritance taxes.

Inquiry: When a current or potential lender looks at your credit report in order to make a credit decision. For example, if you apply for a credit card, the credit card company will make an inquiry, and it will be notated on your credit report. Having too many inquiries listed on your credit report can be negative.

Installment Credit: This is a form of credit where you pay the money owed back in installments. A car loan is an installment loan because you make payments each month.

Interest: With a credit account, this is the charge you pay for the use of the credit, not including additional fees. With savings, this is the money paid to you by the financial institution for depositing your money with their facility.

Intestacy: When someone dies without having specified a beneficiary in a legal will.

Investment Consultant: A professional who assists people in investing their money for the maximum return.

Lender: An individual or organization that lends money, usually with the intention of earning money from the transaction. A credit card company is a lender, but a friend who loans you money may also be considered a lender.

Line of Credit: A credit account that gives borrowers access to a certain amount of money. Payments are only required when there is a balance on the account. As payments are made, the money becomes available for purchases again.

Lump-Sum Distribution: Used to describe when one payment is made instead of several payments. For example, a person who wins the lottery may decide to take one lump-sum distribution instead of receiving annual payments.

Macroeconomics: The study of the economy as a whole.

Matching Contribution: Money that an employer adds to an employee's retirement contribution. This is an attractive benefit offered by employers that can help retirement accounts grow quickly.

Matching Strategy: A strategy used by investment professionals that is designed to schedule investments in the best way to maximize growth.

Microeconomics: The study of portions of the economy instead of analyzing the economy as a whole.

Mortgage Brokers: These professionals act as liaisons between mortgage lenders and potential borrowers. Brokers try to find the best loan product for borrowers based on their eligibility.

Mutual Fund: Instead of investing as an individual, people use mutual funds, or groups of investors, to increase their buying power. These funds combine many people in order to invest.

National Foundation for Consumer Credit: A nonprofit organization that assists consumers who have credit problems. Consumers can get credit counseling as well as help with renegotiating debt through this organization (**www.nfcc.org**).

Non-Sufficient Funds (NSF): Occurs when a check is presented for payment, but there is not enough money in the account to cover the total cost of the check. There are usually costly fees associated with an NSF.

Nonelective Contribution: A contribution that an employer makes to an employee's retirement account as a benefit to the employee.

Paid as Agreed: A positive notation your credit report. This means you are paying your account as you promised.

Passbook: Given to financial intuition customers to record their account transactions. This can be a great way to keep track of spending.

Pension Fund: A type of retirement account provided by an employer, used to build money for the pension plans of employees.

Pension Plan: A retirement account funded by employers.

Perkins Loan: Student loans that are subsidized by the government and are based on the financial needs of the student.

Personal Identification Number (PIN): A secret code to access money from an ATM or to make purchases using a debit card. Your PIN should be unique and should not be shared with other people.

PLUS Loan: A student loan that parents obtain to help fund a child's college-related expenses.

Private Mortgage Insurance (PMI): An additional charge that mortgage companies charge to borrowers who do not make a substantial down payment, usually around 20 percent. This is also called "foreclosure insurance."

Points: A fee that borrowers pay in order to buy the interest rate down on a mortgage loan.

Principal: The total amount you owe on a loan minus any interest and fees not yet charged.

Rate Cap: The preset maximum or minimum percentage that an adjustable rate loan can achieve. For example, an adjustable rate loan with an interest rate of a 6 percent and a cap of +/- 2 percent will never go higher than 8 percent or lower than 4 percent.

Re-age: When a credit account has not had any action for an extended period of time, but then something occurs to make the account active again. For example, if you call and speak to a collector to try to get a payment plan for a debt that you have not paid for several months, the account may be re-aged.

Real Estate Agent: A professional who can help people buy or sell real estate.

Reconciliation: Another word used for balancing a checkbook. Reconciling a bank statement means that you make sure your own records are accurate according to the records sent to you by the financial institution.

Refinancing: The act of obtaining a new loan that pays off an existing loan, preferably at a lower interest rate.

Reverse Mortgage: A type of mortgage only available to seniors. The loan funds are disbursed to the senior, but the loan does not have to be paid back until the borrower moves or dies.

Rollover: Allows a person to move retirement funds from one account to another without any tax penalties. The account holder does not have access to the funds during the rollover.

Roth 401(k): This is a retirement account through an employer that allows people to pay taxes on the contributions now instead of later, which may save money in the long run.

Roth IRA: A retirement account where taxes on the contributions are paid beforehand, which makes the eventual distributions at retirement age not taxable.

Service charge: A fee that is charged for a service. For example, some credit card companies charge a monthly service fee to cardholders.

Stafford Loan: A federally subsidized student loan that is available to college students who attend school at least part-time.

Tax-sheltered: Refers to an account that is not charged full taxes.

Term: The length of time, usually in months, that a loan is amortized to be paid back. For example, most car loans have a term of 60 months.

Treasury Bills (T-Bills): A savings method where you lend a certain amount of money to the government for a certain amount of time in order to receive interest back.

Unified Managed Account (UMA): An investment account that includes several different forms of investments, but are all managed collectively as a whole by a professional.

Withdrawal: Occurs when money is taken out of your account. For example, if you use your debit card to purchase lunch, the amount of the purchase is withdrawn from your account.

Author
Biography

Tamsen Butler is a freelance writer and editor. She is the personal finance blogger for Banks.com, as well as the featured expert for LoveToKnow.com's *Ask the Mortgage Expert*. She has also written for TheBudgetFashionista.com as well as other fun financial sites. She has two vibrant children and stays busy with graduate school, writing, and volunteer work.

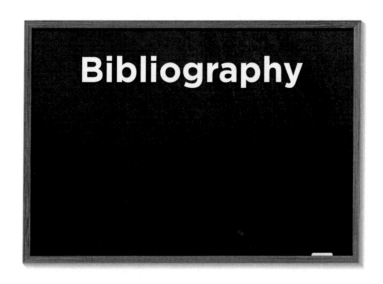

Bibliography

Average Credit Score. Retrieved November 16, 2009 from **www.experian.com/credit-education/average-credit-score.html**.

Budgeting: Making the Most of Your Money. Retrieved November 16, 2006 from **www.moneyandstuff.info/lessons/2CBudgetingSaving_Budgeting.pdf**.

Burrell, Jamaine. *How to Repair Your Credit Score Now: Simple No Cost Methods You Can Put to Use Today.* Atlantic Publishing Company, 2007.

Learn to Budget. Retrieved November 16, 2009 from **http://master.teen.growingmembers.com/Learn_to_Budget_119.html**.

Teen Budget Worksheet. Retrieved November 16, 2009 from **http://printables.familyeducation.com/teen/money-management/57920.html**.

Lipphardt, Debra. *The Scholarship and Financial Aid Solution: How to Go to College for Next to Nothing with Short Cuts, Tricks, and Tips from Start to Finish.* Atlantic Publishing Company, 2008.

More Adult Children Return Home After College – To Stay – This Summer Than Ever Before. Retrieved November 16, 2009 from **www.free-press-release.com/news/200807/1215793534.html**.

Index